Miracles
in the
Liberian Civil War

Miracles
in the
Liberian Civil War

Jonathan S. Morris

ReadersMagnet, LLC

TABLE OF CONTENTS

Foreword..ix

Chapter 1: Background 1

Chapter 2: A Family Divided...............................9

Chapter 3: Inner Turmoil....................................15

Chapter 4: The Miracles Begin 32

Chapter 5: Return Route 40

Chapter 6: Memories, Clans, and Families 52

Chapter 7: Spiritual Warfare.............................60

Chapter 8: Humor and Fear...............................69

Chapter 9: Refuge in the Forest........................74

Chapter 10: Sustained by the Hymns,
            the Word of God, and Nature 89

Chapter 11: Forgiveness 104

Chapter 12: Lessons from the Liberian Civil War........115

Bibliography 127

A thousand shall fall at thy side,
And ten thousand at thy right hand;
But it shall not come nigh thee.

(Psalm 91:7)

FOREWORD

There has never in my life been an opportunity quite like this—to learn about the nation of Liberia, and so up close—as the editor of Morris's first book . Until this assignment, I did not know that the nation of Liberia was founded as a new community for slaves released from the United States long before Lincoln signed the Emancipation Proclamation.

It has been heavy, sad, enlightening, and joyful for me to immerse myself in Jonathan's story, which is God's story in history. I was grateful for every minute and every word in which I could help to document God's miracles along Jonathan's way. My source of passion for this manuscript completely stems from a desire that this testimony be shared, spread out, and used by God to encourage believing or unbelieving people. Messages and lessons exist within these lines that have ability to inform, nourish, and embolden many around the world.

Indeed, "good works were prepared in advance" for Jesus' followers (Ephesians 2:10). It is through testimonies and stories, such as this memoir from Jonathan Morris, that disciples come to understand themselves better, come to understand their callings more acutely, and receive God's power more effectively. Jonathan was very clear throughout our working relationship that no matter what happened with the cropping or revising of this book, the text should focus primarily on God's miracles, God's story. That was paramount in Jonathan's view. Those scenes, which most clearly revealed God's promises as relevant and as applicable to Jonathan personally, should be the most emphasized scenes of all. Jonathan cared that his readers would wrestle with the question: Does God's Word ever apply to me as an individual?

Jonathan's story displays a unique and precious intervention, which God offered to him. I believe that God's Word can hold that kind of power, while it is still very important to me that we humans read the Scriptures in the context of their whole. The dangers of pulling out select verses or of focusing on isolated sentences of the entire Bible are many. It is my solid conviction that the Bible is living and active and that it does speak; it speaks when the entire collection of letters, poems, and dreams are studied in their proper context, and it can sometimes speak when a person randomly or hastily comes to its pages. The apostle Paul, even while writing the New Testament letters, was not in a glass-windowed office, careful to place each letter into its perfect historical setting. He was, most of the time, on a cold prison floor, wearing a rag for a shirt, nursing some large wounds which he had received from recent floggings.

Miracles in the Liberian Civil War, as a word of witness; is important for sedentary academics and for fleeing refugees alike. My prayer is that the readers of this testimony, just as for any readers of the Bible, would approach the pages with a desire to be a humble learner, a desire to quickly confess any of our own sins or blind spots as soon as they are exposed by the Bible text, and a desire to see Jesus and his Gospel, meaning "Good News," within each chapter. Even when there are circumstances in which God does not intervene, does not answer the way we wish, or does not help in the way we expect, his words are still a soothing balm and a solace, "sweeter than honey" (Psalm 19:10). The Scriptures can hint at His presence until we literally feel Him warmly near. Jonathan was polite and appreciative as we communicated back and forth about our different plans or thoughts about the book project. I am thankful I was given the opportunity to surround myself with these pages, these scenes, these stories of God's amazing grace through Jesus Christ.

—Liv Hunziker

CHAPTER 1

Background

My homeland, Liberia, is 43,000 square miles (69,201.8 sq.-km) in land area, and it is situated on the West Coast of Africa, eleven degrees above the equator in the Gulf of Guinea. It is bordered by Sierra Leone on the west, Guinea on the north, Cote d'Ivoire on the east, and on the south, the Atlantic Ocean. The land of Liberia is characterized by mostly flat to rolling coastal plains containing mangrove swamps. There are rolling plateaus and low mountains, rising only in the northeast, while tropical rainforests cover most of the gentle hills in the south.

The Grains Coast, or Pepper Coast, was the name of present-day Liberia before the African-American settlers arrived there. The Pepper Coast received its name from the abundance of meleguetta pepper that was once the primary item of trade between European traders and the indigenous inhabitants along the coast. The pepper was also known as the "grain of paradise," which gave rise to an alternative name, the "Grains Coast."1 The land has always been decked with palm trees from which palm oil and palm butter were extracted for cooking and other uses. The palm trees grew naturally in Liberia, and they belonged to the land, to the community. They were never the possession of any one man, unless they were on private property. Most palm trees were available to the common Liberian man, woman or, child, and passersby could wander up and freely enjoy the fruits straight off of their branches. The palm tree is one of the symbols displayed on the Seal of the Republic of Liberia.

The country has a rich abundance of other natural resources; including diamonds, gold, iron ore, timber, water, and more. Liberia's natural resources can provide for all its citizens; unfortunately, it is one of the poorest, most backward, and underdeveloped nations on the planet. Human and infrastructural developments are at their worst.

The Grains Coast has been inhabited at least as far back as the twelfth century, perhaps earlier. There are sixteen different ethnic tribes inhabiting present-day Liberia, and they include: Gola, Kissi, Bassa, Dei or Dehn, Vai, Kpelle, Lorma, Belle, Gbandi, Gio or Dahn, Mano or Maa, Kru, Grebo, Krahn, Sapo, and Mandingo. The Gola and Kissi are known to have been the earliest inhabitants of the Grain Coast.

Liberia, as a modern principality, was founded by the American Colonization Society (ACS) in 1816 for the resettlement of freed slaves from the United States.2

The first group of freed slaves arrived on the Grain Coast on January 7, 1822 and settled on Providence Island in present-day Monrovia. Those first settlers were frequently called the "freed men of color." They were not freeing as in affordable but free as in emancipated. The English language introduced by the freemen of color is the official language, while nearly twenty indigenous languages are spoken within the country.

Right from the beginning, there was indigenous resistance to the colonization. Allied tribes with combined forces fought desperately to dislodge the settlers in many decisive battles and were defeated. The indigenous people gave in to the settlers and subsequently loss control over their own lands and became the most exploited and oppressed layers of the population for 133 years.

The free slaves extended their settlement and occupied Cape Mesurado which is present-day Monrovia. They named the city "Christopolis", meaning "city of Christ". In 1824, Christopolis was renamed Monrovia, in honor of James Monroe, fifth President of the United States. Those immigrants, all freed slaves from the United States, formed a colony; the American colonization Society (ACS) appointed Jehudi Ashmun, a white American of European descent, as its first agent to manage the new colony. Ashmun initiated an expansion effort that increased the territory of the colony by purchases and treaties with the indigenous people. He worked to create a structure to govern the colony, and increased agricultural production, which led to increased trade and interaction between the colonists and their indigenous neighbors. Ashmun had a dream to create an American empire in Africa. However, Ashmun died in 1828 after a brief illness from malaria without fulfilling his dream. Liberia would have been a success story had Ashmun lived to fulfill his dream.

A constitution was then written to guide the new nation. Harvard University Professor Simeon Greenleaf crafted the document, modeling it after the United States Constitution. The commonwealth declared its independence from any western powers on July 26, 1847. They gave their commonwealth the name "The Republic of Liberia" and crafted a motto: "The love of liberty brought us here." Joseph Jenkins Roberts was elected as the first president of the Republic of Liberia in 1848. Liberia became the first independent black republic in Africa and the only African nation, aside from Ethiopia, which had never experienced the influence of colonialists directly out of the European continent.

The original settlers and their descendants, who became known as America-Liberians, dominated the political, social, and economic landscape of the new nation and largely excluded the indigenous population from the country's affairs for over 133 years after independence. On April 12, 1980, a master sergeant with the Armed Forces of Liberia (AFL), Samuel Kanyon Doe, from the indigenous Krahn ethnic group, led a military coup and overthrew the government, killing then President William R. Tolbert, Jr. 4. The Doe regime was quickly found to be corrupt and repressive. Doe consolidated power by eliminating his associates one by one until only a few remained alive. He had a new constitution written, replacing Harvard University Professor Greenleaf's document that had governed the country since her independence. A timetable was set for new elections to be held in 1985, hoping to place power back in the hands of the indigenous groups who had lived on the land before the freed slaves returned to Africa.

The ironic stipulation was that Doe would be the new president. Doe won the presidential elections with a landslide victory on October 15, 1985 in an election process, which many international observers (though not the US) dubbed fraudulent. The opposition cried foul— primarily due to the high number of ballots which were never even counted—and called for a re-election. The government of the United States confirmed the election results as credible and blamed the reported irregularities on the country's high rate of illiteracy.

On the morning of November 12, 1985, the Liberian people were awakened by the playing of the national anthem. The custom had been that before the Liberian president would give a speech the national anthem must be played first; then the next voice was that of the president of the Republic of Liberia. Samuel Doe, in particular, was fond of the national anthem that made him feel imperial in his presidency.

In President Samuel Kanyon Doe's Liberia and prior, the national radio station, ELBC, opened in the morning with the playing of the National Anthem and closed at midnight with the anthem as well. Upon hearing the anthem that early hour of the morning, people thought that it was the regular playing of the anthem for the beginning of a normal working day, and they may have been expecting the voice that would follow would be that of CIC, Dr. Samuel Kanyon Doe. No. It was the voice of General Thomas G. Quiwonkpa, the former commanding general of the Armed Forces of Liberia, a fellow coup maker with Samuel Doe with whom he had fallen out and had fled in exile.

General Quiwonkpa announced to the nation that he, with his National Patriotic Forces under his command, had overthrown the government of President Samuel Kanyon Doe and that Samuel Doe was in hiding though there was no escape for him. He assured the nation of a nonviolent coup in which there would be no bloodshed. The Liberian people were still angered by the October 15, 1985 presidential election that was rigged by President Doe and endorsed by the United States, so they greeted the news with excitement and took to the streets in jubilation.

The jubilation came to an abrupt end by two p.m. on the same day, when the national anthem was back on the air. This time, it was not the excited voice of General Quiwonkpa but the quivering and broken voice of CIC Dr. Samuel Kanyon Doe, announcing that Quiwonkpa's coup has failed; and the general and his National Patriotic Forces were on the run, a price that the citizens of Nimba County paid dearly with their lives, unfortunately. Forces loyal to Samuel Doe inflicted unimaginable violence on the people of Nimba County, which was General

Quiwonkpa's home county. The general was captured and killed, along with prominent citizens of the county and families, friends, and acquaintances of the coup makers. The violence inflicted by the Doe government, as a reprisal against the failed coup, set the stage for the brutal civil war that destroyed this once peaceful and vibrant nation.

On December 24, 1989, the National Patriotic Front of Liberia (NPFL), a rebel group led by former civil servant Charles M. Taylor, invaded the country and attempted to oust Doe's governing regime. Taylor had allegedly lost favor with Doe's government in the 1980s, being imprisoned in the United States where he allegedly broke out of jail and resurfaced in Libya. He then trained Liberian and other West African dissidents, forming a fierce guerrilla movement designed to invade Liberia and oust Samuel Doe from power.

The government of Liberia, under Doe's leadership, responded to Taylor's "Bloody Rebellion" by deploying AFL troops to north eastern Liberia. As fighting continued between Doe's AFL and Taylor's NPFL, the Liberian government didn't provide protection to the citizens of Liberia. Instead, the AFL offered loyalty only to Doe's cabinet and members of the Krahn or Mandingo ethnic groups. Doe came from the Krahn people, and Mandingos happened to be the only other ethnic group that allied with Doe at the time. Taylor's rebels, on the other hand, killed any Liberian government officials and any members of Doe's political party. His "freedom fighters" were also targeting and killing Krahns, Mandingos, and others who stood in opposition to Taylor's Bloody Rebellion.

Ethnic groups, tribal loyalties, and Americo-Liberians existed all the time, but they became even more sectarian and divisive when the civil war broke out in the late 1980s. Complex webs of revenge and memory made the lush lands of Liberia into a tapestry of strife and bloodshed, with most of the conflicts rooted in a person's ethnic heritage.

Liberia had been a beautiful country, and the people were relatively peaceful until Doe, Taylor, and the first civil war erupted in 1989 to shatter the calm. Many believe that Liberia's golden days are cemented in the past.

CHAPTER 2

A Family Divided

Government officials, members of the Krahn and Mandingo groups and other targeted citizens were being executed in rebel-controlled areas. Rebels and the other ethnic groups were being killed in AFL-controlled areas. As fighting intensified, rumors began circulating in my neighborhood.

The rumors gave the impression that Taylor declared that his forces would not attack the Firestone Rubber Plantation Company. Firestone owned and operated one million acres of Liberia's farmland and had produced natural rubber since 1926. Its plantation headquarters were in the city of Harbel, about thirty miles east of Monrovia. In the Liberia of 1989, and still today, civilians were not always informed adequately by their government regarding current issues that might directly affect their daily lives. Rumors, substantiated or unsubstantiated, were the only means by which citizens could become aware of any current events. Rumors thrived in Liberia during the civil war.

Another rumor spread word that the US Embassy in Monrovia declared that if the NPFL attacked Monrovia, fighting would last in that city for only ten days. Therefore, based on that rumor, the embassy advised citizens to store enough food and water in their homes for a maximum of ten days.

Citizens received the first rumor, regarding the safety of Firestone with excitement, thinking that Harbel would be the best place of refuge in the nation at that time. Citizens and foreign residents alike bought into the story, so families from Monrovia and other parts of the country were relocated to Harbel from the middle of April until the first week of June, 1990.

My family was living in Monrovia, the capital city of Liberia by early 1990, where I had a job within the government's National Social Security and Welfare Corporation where I served in a middle management capacity. My family has been Seventh-Day Adventists, and at that time, we had our membership with the Paynesville Seventh-Day Adventist Church located in the northern suburb of Monrovia. I also served as a local elder there.

I bought into the "news" myself. When my cousin, who lived in Harbel with her family, came to Monrovia and offered to take my wife and children to her home because Harbel would be safe, I accepted without a second thought. We had three very small children at the time. We bought into the US Embassy rumor also, so I thought I could live and manage myself in Monrovia, bear the tensions of war, and subsist easily on the little food and water that I had stored for up to ten days. Without intending to, I had torn my family apart and had distanced myself from them in a time of war and uncertainty, keeping only my younger brother with me. It was a grave mistake indeed! The lesson learned in retrospect is that in times of emergency, war or famine, every family should remain together and travel together as much as is humanly possible.

Three weeks after separating from my wife and infants, I resolved to visit them with a small bit of food and to assess their housing and safety needs in Harbel. I took a taxi cab from Paynesville Red Light and got to Fifteen Gate on the Monrovia-Kakata highway arriving at around seven o'clock P.M. Government soldiers stationed at Fifteen Gate stopped our taxi and ordered everybody to exit the cab and approach a checkpoint by foot, leaving only the cab driver and all of our belongings behind. There had been seven of us in the taxi: three men, three women, and a child. After we had crossed the checkpoint, those who were identified as Mandingos and any women and children were allowed to re-enter the taxi and resume their journeys. The adult males and non-Mandingos were prevented from leaving the gate area. I began to feel a growing darkness and a chilling anxiety.

As more vehicles arrived at Fifteen Gate, the soldiers did the same thing; they stopped the vehicles, ordered everyone down to cross the checkpoint, and required any adult non-Mandingo males to stay. At that point in Liberian history, only the Mandingos, women, and children were allowed to travel freely around the "free land" known as Liberia. By eight o'clock, the soldiers were drunk, bullying anyone nearby. None of them could communicate to us the reason we were being detained at Fifteen Gate. Whenever more vehicles were stopped, then more bewildered, trapped males were added to our number. We began to ask individual soldiers who appeared somewhat friendly what was happening, but they would not say anything. A fellow traveller said to us that they may kill us that night to report to Monrovia that we were rebels. The Liberian government soldiers at that time often killed civilian males; they allegedly carried false reports to the senior military commanders that those killed were rebels. At that time what the soldiers reported from the battlefront was never verified for its authenticity.

By that time, I was terrified and confused. I thought to myself that I may never see my wife and children again. I began to pray, "O God, help me. O God, deliver me." I tried to come up with a way of escape since the area was familiar to me. Yet there were no escape routes as the armed soldiers and heavy weapons were strategically placed all around. Those soldiers, fearfully dressed, were intentionally appearing awful and terrifying. In all my life, I have never seen Liberian soldiers who seemed quite that ominous-looking—very much like monsters. I began to wonder where President Doe could have found them. They were tall and unusually dark. An average Liberian male would have been of medium height, with a much lighter complexion than the monster-like soldiers I saw before me. They spoke little to no English, and I could only assume they were French-speaking Krahns from the Ivory Coast. Doe was Krahn, and Liberia has common border with Cote d'Ivoire (Ivory Coast), and both countries have Krahns within both sides of their borders.

At about nine that night, a pickup truck traveling from Monrovia to Kakata came to the Fifteen Gate and was ordered to stop. The soldiers ordered every passenger to step down and walk through the checkpoint to be screened. The occupants were all Mandingo men, women, and children, so they had freedom of passage. When they had crossed the checkpoint, the Mandingo men, women, and children were allowed back in their pickup truck to continue their trip. As the passengers began climbing into the pickup, I inched close enough to quietly climb on board. As I attempted to climb the Mandingo car, a boy asked me if I was Mandingo. Though I was not, I murmured yes.

The lad allowed me to board the truck; he pressured me to be swift since the vehicle wanted to get away from that evil place. Only a few seconds later, the engine was started. And we drove away. My body released an unconscious sigh of relief. I silently thanked God for my deliverance. I asked God to protect all those I had left behind. I am still profoundly grateful to that Mandingo boy for allowing me to board the truck. As I looked back and saw the distance increasing between myself and Fifteen Gate, I found myself drinking in and gasping large breaths of air, life, and relief. I was praying also that no one should discover my true identity that I was not a Mandingo because I wasn't sure what reaction to expect. A way to find that out would have been by simply speaking Mandingo to me and expecting me to respond in Mandingo. I would have failed miserably because I knew not a word of Mandingo apart from counting from one to ten in Mandingo, which I learned from my father's Mandingo customers who counted their goods (cola nuts) before they bought them. Counting one to ten in Mandingo goes like this: kiliŋ (1), fula (2), saba (3), naani (4), luulu (5), wooro (6), worowula (7), sey (8), kononto (9), and tan (10). But's all I know in Mandingo. Fortunately, no one examined or tested my Mandingo legitimacy. They merely chatted and laughed with one another in their tongue, carefree, as though nothing out of the ordinary was taking place in Liberia. They accommodated me.

They continued talking among themselves until we arrived in Kakata. When the truck had stopped, I reached into my pocket, paid the carboy, and thanked him for his kindness. I spent the night in Kakata. The next morning, without going on to Harbel or seeing my beloved family, I returned to Monrovia. I decided to make no further attempts to visit Firestone or my family until I received the next piece of news.

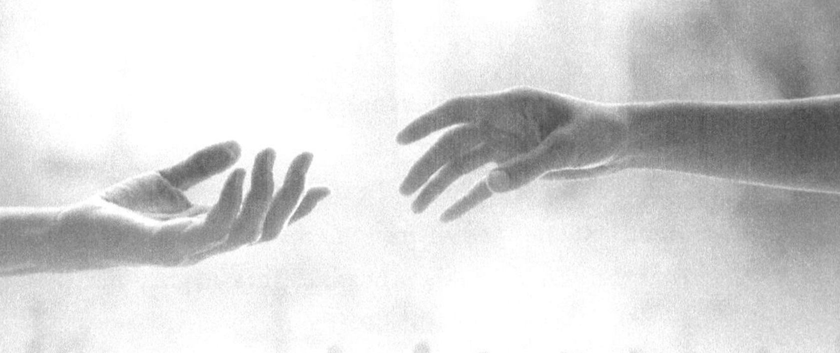

CHAPTER 3

Inner Turmoil

On June 5, 1990, NPFL rebels attacked the Firestone Plantation Company, killing hundreds and wounding dozens in the city of Harbel. This was broadcasted all over Monrovia by the international media—the British Broad Casting Corporation (BBC), Voice of America (VOA), Radio Deutsche Welle of Germany, and other news networks. News from the Liberian Broad Casting Corporation (ELBC), the Liberian national radio station, was highly censored, and its news about the war was considered by many as not credible.

Shortly after international media broke the story, the streets of Monrovia were unusually bare because the people had heard solid news that Firestone had indeed been attacked. Only the voices of people weeping and wailing in their homes could be heard in communities and neighborhoods whose family members had left to move to Harbel weeks earlier. The streets of Monrovia were virtually emptied of people.

Charles Taylor had compromised his integrity by going back on his promise. The people felt as though doomsday had come. Every neighborhood groaned under the chorus of anguished cries and distressed voices. I saw women putting their hands on their heads as they shouted out names of family members who they thought may have been killed. I, too, grieved and wept for my family in Harbel, not only for my wife and children but also for my sisters, brothers, nephews, and nieces who had congregated in there.

I resolved to take the risk and make another trip there, but such a trip was not possible on a week day while I was scheduled for work. June 5 was on a Tuesday, and the government backlash was already underway, lasting throughout the ensuing weeks, hunting for those not aligned with the AFL, or for anyone who was suspect.

Meanwhile, civil servants were still required to report to work daily and on time. I was a government employee in a middle management position at the National Social Security and Welfare Corporation. It was difficult for a civil servant to leave work for even a day with or without excuse. When the excuse was approved by a supervisor, it was still subject to heavy scrutiny. Though not explicitly stated, an employee's absence for even one day was recorded as abandonment, which could be interpreted by government security forces (planted in various offices) as disloyalty. Disloyalty was treated as defection or as an affiliation with Taylor's NPFL rebels. And whenever the authorities felt that way about a civil servant, proof or no proof, that citizen could soon "disappear."

Civil servants quickly learned they needed to be very careful as the rebels were drawing nearer to Monrovia. We reported to work, and we were supposed to act and behave as if there was no trouble in the country and that everything was normal. The government of Liberia remained in a constant state of denial, advising citizens to remain calm, communicating that government security forces were in control of the situation. Meanwhile, the government had warned that any person who said there was a rebel somewhere would be arrested. They had to produce the rebel or he or she would be treated as one. All the while, rebel forces were drawing closer and closer to our nation's capital.

Not a day passed after the June 5 attack, when I wasn't flooded with worry for my family. I ached to rush to Harbel to try seeing them, yet with the dire situation and the work stipulations, I didn't understand any way for me to break away. This led to some precarious hours at the work place, when my performance very well could have been called into question; my mind was so consumed with my family and all of the unknowns that I had a difficult time focusing on quality work.

I finally made up my mind that on the next weekend, I would again attempt the trek to the war front, Harbel, to search for my family. When the weekdays were finished, there would be no need for a supervisor to approve or unapproved my absence. I wouldn't need to make excuses for myself. The weekends were mine; only then I was my own man. I knew with my whole being. I had to visit Harbel, even if it meant I'd never return to work.

On Saturday June 9, I attended a church service in my local Seventh - day Adventist church. Before the service began, I informed the pastor of my situation, and I asked for prayer. During the service, I was prayed for with the laying on of hands by our pastor and elders. After that prayer, I felt confident that the Lord would indeed protect me on my journey to Harbel and back again. Moreover, I received an outpouring of support, encouragement, and comforting words from most but not all of the other church members.

I could not bear even the slightest possibility of believing I had lost my family in a war like the Liberian Civil War; a war with no moral backing and no just cause. I exercised disbelief whenever the thought of their demise found occasion to trouble my mind. My kids were too young to be abandoned as casualties or be included in the death statistics of the Liberian civil war. I couldn't even fathom the thought. My two-year-old, one-and-a-half-year-old, nine-month-old baby, and my wife were priceless and precious to me. I loved them.

Thus I began on Saturday night, June 9, 1990 by reading Scripture and singing hymns until morning broke. My younger brother, Alfred, who had remained with me in Monrovia, was also in the house. I didn't invite him to remain awake with me as I prayed since he was able to sleep and because I felt so deeply confused. I also, like the patriarch Jacob upon reaching the river Jabboh, sent his family ahead in order to be with the Lord one-on-one, wanted to be alone with the Lord to pour out my heart and grieve before him. I couldn't do that with a boy sitting with me all night. He may not understand. So he slept peacefully in the other room, even knowing that he'd journey with me the next day. Before night fell, I told him that he would accompany me the next morning to Harbel. My father once told me when I was young that a man should not cry or weep in front of women or children, especially his daughters. If man must weep, he must do so in private and in isolation where no one would see or notice him. That advice came because I was accustomed to leaving the playground crying and coming home whenever I was among my peers. He did not hesitate to send me back to that playground, especially when I had sustained no apparent injury.

When I started to pray through the evening, I petitioned the Lord first to forgive my sins and iniquities. The Bible says that "if we claim that we have not sinned, we make him out to be a liar, and his word is not in us" (John 1:10). I petitioned the Lord also to have mercy on me and on my family. The Lord had said, "I will have mercy on whom I will have mercy, and I will have compassion on whom I will have compassion" (Exodus 33:19; Romans 9:15). I needed that grace, I needed that mercy, and I needed that compassion, so I said: "Oh, God. I don't deserve it, but please let me be one of those to whom you will be gracious and on whom you will show mercy and compassion!"

I needed God to shield and defend me while I travelled unarmed to the battle front of the NPFL and AFL and to pass through their war machines. Those two notorious forces of evil, equally vicious and atrocious, had wreaked such havoc on the citizens of Liberia that everyone feared and abhorred them. In their advancing, neither group had shown any regard for civilian well-being—neither group had ever spared a captured POW.

Even though both sides had occasionally captured victims, and both sides had had portions of the enemy force surrender to them in a battle, not a single life was spared by the NPFL or the AFL. They murdered each fighting man that surrendered and was disarmed. They treated those forces that surrendered as if they were some aliens from space or non-Liberians. Soon, when both sides realized this, they decided to just continue fighting, even when it seemed wiser to surrender. They'd just fought onward to preserve one more day of life or to at least die through honest fighting. Chances would be slim for civilians, like me, to live past the NPFL or the AFL since I was a non-Krahn, non-Gio, and non-Mano, and I couldn't feign any of their languages. To get past either monster, I would need to invoke all the powers of God and heaven. But first I needed to make sure I prayed the prayer for personal forgiveness and cleansing. I found that prayer in Psalm 51, a Psalm of David. Aloud I slowly read:

Have mercy upon me, O God, according to thy loving-kindness: according unto the multitude of thy tender mercies blot out my transgressions. 2 Wash me thoroughly from mine iniquity, and cleanse me from my sin. For I acknowledge my transgressions: and my sin is ever before me. 4. Against thee, thee only, have I sinned, and done this evil in thy sight: that thou mightiest be justified when thou speakest, and be clear when thou judgest.5 Behold, I was sharpen in iniquity; and in sin did my mother conceive me. 6 Behold, thou desirest truth in the inward parts: and in the hidden part thou shalt make me to know wisdom.7 Purge me with hyssop, and I shall be clean: wash me, and I shall be whiter than snow.8 Make me to hear joy and gladness; that the bones which thou hast broken may rejoice. 9 Hide thy face from my sins, and blot out all mine iniquities.10 Create in me a clean heart, O God; and renew a right spirit within me.11Cast me not away from thy presence; and take not thy Holy Spirit from me. 12 Restore unto me the joy of thy salvation; and uphold me with thy free Spirit. 13 Then will I teach transgressors thy ways; and sinners shall be converted unto thee. 14 Deliver me from blood-guiltiness, O God, thou God of my salvation: and my tongue shall sing aloud of thy righteousness. 15 O Lord, open thou my lips; and my mouth shall show forth thy praise. 16 For thou desirest not sacrifice; else would I give it: thou delightest not in burnt offering. 17 The sacrifices of God are a broken spirit: a broken and a contrite heart, O God, thou wilt not despise.18 Do good in thy good pleasure unto Zion: build thou the walls of Jerusalem.19 Then shalt thou be pleased with the sacrifices of righteousness, with burnt offering and whole burnt offering: then shall they offer bullocks upon thine alter." (Psalm 51:1–19)

I then confessed any and all of my sins that I could remember because "if we claim we have not sinned, we make him out to be a liar and his Word is not in us" (John 1:10). While, "If we confess our sins, he is faithful and just to forgive us our sins and to cleanse us from all unrighteousness" (John 1:9). Having said that prayer, I felt that my sins, past and present, were indeed forgiven and that I could come clean and boldly before God's throne of grace to ask for the deliverance I so desperately needed. I then read Psalm 91 aloud:

He that dwelleth in the secret place of the most High shall abide under the shadow of the Almighty. **2** I will say of the Lord, He is my refuge and my fortress: my God; in him will I trust. **3** Surely he shall deliver thee from the snare of the fowler, and from the noisome pestilence. **4** He shall cover thee with his feathers, and under his wings shalt thou trust: his truth shall be thy shield and buckler. **5** Thou shalt not be afraid for the terror by night; nor for the arrow that flieth by day; **6** Nor for the pestilence that walketh in darkness; nor for the destruction that wasteth at noonday. **7** A thousand shall fall at thy side, and ten thousand at thy right hand; but it shall not come nigh thee. **8** Only with thine eyes shalt thou behold and see the reward of the wicked.**9** Because thou hast made the Lord, which is my refuge, even the most High, thy habitation; **10** There shall no evil befall thee, neither shall any plague come nigh thy dwelling. **11** For he shall give his angels charge over thee, to keep thee in all thy ways. **12** They shall bear thee up in their hands, lest thou dash thy foot against a stone. **13** Thou shalt tread upon the lion and adder: the young lion and the dragon shalt thou trample under feet. **14** Because he hath set his love upon me, therefore will I deliver him: I will set him on high, because he hath known my name.**15** He shall call upon me, and I will answer him: I will be with him in trouble; I will deliver him, and honor him. **16** With long life will I satisfy him, and show him my salvation.

When I had finished reading that passage, all of my fears and anxiety vanished. I gained more courage, and my faith was strengthened. I believed that my sins were certainly forgiven and that the Lord would protect and lead me to Harbel and that I would discover my family still safe and healthy.

This Psalm formed the basis of my faith and courage that made it possible to make my rescue trip to Harbel. I was especially touched by verse seven: "A thousand shall fall at thy side, ten thousand at thy right hand, but it shall not come nigh thee." I murmured to myself, "This is it! This is the verse for me." As the twilight hours expanded, I analyzed and worked through that one verse. I repeated it, again and again. "A thousand shall fall at thy side, ten thousand at thy right hand, but it shall not come nigh thee." Then I paraphrased the text and put it within the context of my own situation. "A thousand bullets and hand grenades shall fall at my side, and ten thousand at my right hand, but they shall not come near me." Then I analyzed the text and rationalized the result and in the following way: I said to myself, bullets that are flying around do not come in their thousands; and not even in their hundreds at any one time, even when fired from a machine gun. Likewise, the hand grenades exploding here and there do not occur in their thousands at any one time, either, even when fired from a rocket launcher. The most bullets discharged at any one time is when they are fired from a machine gun, but even at that, they never come in their hundreds at any single moment. The rebels did not have a sophisticated weapon system at all.

Therefore, I concluded that if the word of God says a thousand of any harmful object shall fall at my side and ten thousand at my right hand and shall not come near me, how is it possible these bullets and grenades that could come in twos and threes or at most, dozens or so, would come near me? My faith to trek to the battle front in Harbel, where an inferno was on display daily, found its basis in Psalm 91:7. I then consoled myself with the thought that of one thousand any weapon directed at me could not come near me, how possible would it be, with God on my side, for a couple of bullets and grenades coming in twos or threes or even tens at any one time would even touch me or come near me? God gave assurance to those that believe and trust in his word that no weapons form against them shall prosper (Isaiah 54:7), and I believe it. I praised God, and I honored God's word because it is fulfilling. The Liberian civil war experience made me to believe so.

As I was praying, I again spoke calmly into the darkness, "This is the Bible verse for me—Psalm 91:7!" I read other Scriptural texts until about twelve A.M., Sunday morning. I also got down on my knees to pray. After just a few minutes on my knees in quiet prayer, I heard a loud explosion and thunderous sounds of artillery coming from the direction of Harbel. The sounds became louder and more terrifying. I became afraid and knew that I could soon lose my new faith!

I heard voices of accusations in my ear, saying I couldn't claim the promises of Psalm 91:7 because those words were not intended for me, Jonathan Morris. Scenes of past mistakes that I had made began to flash across my mind. I instantly lost the belief that "a thousand would fall at my side and ten thousand at my right hand but they would not come near me." Those scenes and doubts all came from Satan, who was a liar from the beginning. He accused me of having committed this error or that error and tried convincing me that I was not worthy of the promises of God. The voice of Satan said that my family members had already been killed and that if I were to travel to Harbel, then I would be killed, too.

At that point I crumbled under the deceit, and I mentally cancelled the trip. I went to my brother's room and roused him from a deep sleep. I told him the trip to Harbel was cancelled. "Why?" he mumbled. "Because I changed my mind. Could you join a final prayer for guidance, with me? I was disappointed; my brother wouldn't even open his eyes to help me pray. I abandoned any more thoughts of prayer, went to bed, and knew nothing more until three A.M., when it felt as though someone had touched me to wake me up.

The Bible verse came to me the moment when I rose to my feet was John 3:16. "For God so loved the world that he gave his only begotten son that whosoever believeth in him should not perish but have everlasting life." I thought to myself; if God sent his Son to the world to die for the sins of the world, I am one of the sinners for whom he died. Then my sins should be covered. I said to myself, I can claim all the promises God made in the Bible because I am one of those for whom Christ came into the world and for whom he died. I felt an assurance, then, that I was covered under the promise. Therefore, I am included in the promise that says "A thousand shall fall at thy side, and ten thousand at thy right hand, but it shall not come nigh thee" (Psalm 91:1). I put my first name in that text read thus: A thousand shall fall at Jonathan's side and ten thousand at his right hand but it shall not come near him. I recited this key verse aloud once more, and my faith was restored. I was confident again that I could make my risky trip and that nothing tragic would happen to me. At that moment, excited, I started shouting in my room, saying "Yes, I am covered, yes I am covered; I can claim all the promises of God in his word!"

I went quickly back to my brother's room and woke him up again, still shouting "I am covered!" He was sitting on his bed, looking at me as though something was wrong with me. I told him that we would go to Harbel in the morning and that we should both be prepared to leave at six. He protested, "But, brother, you said that we weren't going." I told him that yes I said it, but that I changed my mind again. I fled his room and went into mine to continue my prayer, scripture reading, and hymns. That night before dawn, I had discovered powerful scriptural texts and hymns, which would carry me through the entire first Liberian Civil War.

Whenever I was scared or terrified later on in the journey, those very scriptures served to take away my fears. When I was hungry, where there was no food, the hymns and scriptures kept me going as if I had eaten a balanced meal? It was the redemptive love of Jesus Christ that saved wretches like all of us from death. Death was near to my family through the carnage unleashed upon our country by hardened men who did not come to redeem us because we were not in bondage but came for their own personal aggrandizement.

Through that long, difficult Saturday night, I became even more appreciative of Christ's offer to save the world and to save me, Jonathan Morris. My brother and I departed from Monrovia at six on Sunday morning. A taxi brought us (once again) to Fifteen Gate on the Monrovia-Kakata highway. The prayer which I continued chanting in my mind during that frightening taxi ride was that God should not let us see any rebels. I said, "Please, God; do not let any rebels see us but drive them from out path. Again and again, on and on. Fifteen Gates was the halting point for our first leg; all northbound vehicles trying to reach

Kakata and any eastbound vehicles heading toward Harbel had to stop and return to Monrovia.

There were only ten or fifteen AFL soldiers at Fifteen Gate that Sunday morning, compared to the dozens who stood watch when I made my first failed attempt to pass through. A soldier explained to us that many of the other guards had to be rearranged and redeployed due to the recent attacks on Harbel. My brother and I quietly decided together that our next step should be to visit Bahr Town where our parents lived on the farm. Surely my wife and children must have fled Harbel when Firestone was attacked and went to Bahr Town, I thought. It would have been perfect place my family would naturally go, but she did not. If we wanted to reach Bahr Town, which meant possible encounters with various NPF rebel groups. We would need to avoid highways as much as we could. Attempting to appear that we were strolling back to Monrovia, we left Fifteen Gate as discretely as possible and walked a mile or so north, turned onto a bush road at Number Seven, a town about a mile and half north of Fifteen Gate along the Monrovia-Kakata Highway to the interior, and safely stepped into Bahr Town just before two in the afternoon.

My joy was quickly dispelled when I discovered that my wife and children had not yet arrived in Bahr Town. With a sinking stomach and racing heart, I decided to continue on to Harbel. My brother would remain in Bahr Town while my nephew would journey forward with me. My parents warned me that I ought to spend the night and leave early the next morning. The best time to travel through rebel areas was during early morning hours.

"Son, when the sun gets hot, the rebels get hungrier to kill even more people." Gratefully, I accepted my parents' advice and spent the night in Bahr Town. Lying awake for a few hours that night, I mused until I reached a security plan for my nephew and I—just to get through the next leg of the journey. My nephew was a good companion to have for that leg, since he was fluent in the Gio and Mano tongues. Gio and Mano were the primary languages spoken by NPFL forces. My nephew's father was from the Mano ethnic group and had taken him as a four-year-old to the father's hometown, where Gio and Mano were primarily spoken, in Nimba County. My nephew remained in that part of Nimba County until him reached the age of twelve. Part of our safety plan involved taking my government employee ID card with us to display whenever we encountered AFL government forces. The other safety measure was to have this boy with me who spoke Gio and Mano to put us in good favor if we encountered any NPFL rebel groups.

After a very early devotional time, my nephew and I left Bahr Town on foot at five-thirty Monday morning. I had the assurance from God's Word that I'd make it safely to Harbel and back. I had read the Psalms and had believed in the word of God. "A thousand may fall at your side; ten thousand at your right hand, but it will not come near you" (Psalm 91:7). Understandably, it was difficult for my parents to let me continue on, because of the reported atrocities already being committed by the NPFL rebels. The morning was cool, and the sky was clear as the glowing sunrise lightened the eastern sky. The grass was wet with the morning dew as if it had just rained. The daylight was reminiscent of any normal dawn of the past, when there had been no trouble in our land.

As our journey progressed, the atmosphere became tense and haunting. Gun sounds were heard from the vicinity of Harbel, and the shots grew louder as each of our footsteps brought us closer. At this point, only a person with immense courage or with ardent faith in God's Word would dare to proceed further. I was determined, with God as my helper, to make it to the end and back.

My father and some of his Bahr Town neighbors had cautioned me never to expose my government working ID card or any other personal items to any rebels, or I'd be instantly executed. So I bandaged my ID card onto one thigh, bandaged my watch onto the other thigh, and had my clothing over top of them. Unfortunately, after some walking, the metal watch began cutting into my leg. It hurt more and more, soon becoming so painful I couldn't handle it. My nephew and I finally had to stop walking, so I could take all of the metal pieces and bandages off of my skin. By that point I didn't care anymore if the rebels found my valuables. They could do what they wished—I needed to stop the cutting!

We walked through the whole morning and arrived on the edge of Division Forty-Five by early afternoon, Monday June 11, 1990.

Firestone operated on one million acres of Liberia's farmland, and the plantation is divided into forty-five divisions, from Division 1 to 45. Each division had its own camp, where the employees of that division lived and worked. Harbel happened to be the plantation headquarters, situated within Division Forty-Five. During the entire morning hike, the weather and the atmosphere had been peaceful and calm. We had heard shooting but it was never too close to us. Moreover, we did not once see any AFL forces or any NPFL forces with our own eyes. Praise God!

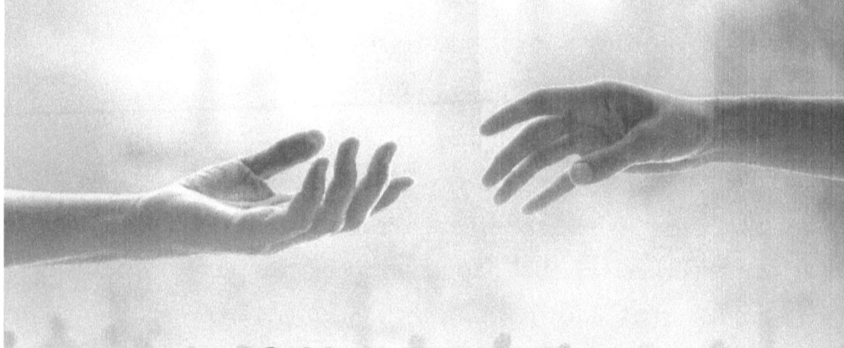

CHAPTER 4

The Miracles Begin

A couple of minutes after we first set foot on Division Forty-Five of the Plantation, sporadic shooting became intense shooting, quite close to us. A few minutes after that, all hell broke loose. Every moment, a new stray bullet was dashing just past our heads, until I motioned to my nephew that we needed to lay flat on our stomachs. Surrounding us in the dirt to our left and to our right laid the bodies of the dead. Several dozen dead men were strewn under the rubber trees filled with bullet wounds. Some appeared to have been killed many hours earlier, some just minutes earlier; fresh blood was still trickling from the bullet gashes. Others appeared to be in early and late stages of decomposing; they must have been killed a few days before. The whole region was filled with a pungent stench. I had never been so close to a dead body before. The Gola and Kpelle culture, in which I was raised, did not permit children to see a corpse, not even if it was the dead body of their mother or father.

Sadly, there I lay with my thirteen-year-old nephew, in a deep pile of dead and slain men. Bullets continued to zip over our heads; they cut branches and limbs off of the nearby rubber trees. Twigs and arms of trees fell by our sides. I've never heard the sound of live bullets before this time, but some bullets flew so close to our ears we could hear the sound "feen," "feen," "feen!" We were terrified.

Throughout our trek to Harbel, I had been reciting Psalm 91. I had memorized the passage while I was an elementary school student at the Presbyterian Mission School a mile and half south of Bahr Town. That school laid the foundation of my Bible knowledge. I chose Psalm 91 for my "key passage" for this journey through the back roads of Liberia. I spoke verse seven aloud as I walked that Monday morning; if anyone passed us, they would have seen me chanting loudly into the sky and would have wondered if I was insane. Sometimes I voiced it out and other times I only moved my lips. "A thousand shall fall at thy side," and I went on and on until the entire chapter was finished then I repeated it.

While we waited there, stretched out on our stomachs, I slowly slipped one hand into my pocket and managed to peek at my watch. It was two in the afternoon. I also carefully opened my Bible that had been in my hand all day and opened to Psalm 91:7. Silently, I drank in those precious words again: "A thousand shall fall at thy side, ten thousand at thy right hand, but it will not come nigh you." I repeated this voice because it was my source of strength and encouragement.

The Holy Bible came as a gift from God to man; once again, its Word was fulfilled in one man's life. The dozens of bullets that were flying overhead and past our sides had not touched us once. The limbs and branches of the trees, which the bullets had sliced off, had fallen all around us, but we were not harmed in any way. God's Word can be trusted. God honors his Word! I closed the Bible and my eyes and prayed, "Lord, we have come this far, please do not let us now return or go back to Monrovia without seeing my family—or without knowing what has happened to them. Please let there be a ceasefire to enable me to go into Harbel to search for my wife and children, my sisters and brothers, and my nephews and nieces. Amen!"

After that amen, there were five minutes filled with noise and violence. Then the guns became silent, all at once. It became very quiet, until the birds that were in shock from the cacophony of bullets just flew back into their trees and began singing. The breeze started to blow, gently moving the rubber leaves as if greeting and encouraging all of us who were below. As I lay there, reflecting on that frightening moment, the second verse of the hymn, "How Great Thou Art" came to my mind and I began humming it in a very low tune:

When through the woods and forest glades I wander. And hear the Birds sing sweetly in the trees. When I look down from lofty mountain grandeur; and hear the brook, and feel the gentle breeze. Chorus: Then sings my soul, my savior God to Thee.

How great Thou art! How great Thou art!

Then sings my soul, my Saviour God, to Thee, How great Thou art! How great Thou art!

We were still lying flat on our stomachs and surrounded by the corpses. My nephew, brave and inquisitive, stood up onto his feet first. Cautiously, I also rose to my feet. We began our walk toward the town. My nephew wanted to walk fast, but I gripped him by the shirt and held him tightly, stopping him. I whispered that we'd need to wait and observe who was actually in control before we moved in.

While waiting in our frozen stance, we saw soldiers dressed in what appeared to be the AFL military uniform. They were walking from house to house, carrying loads of heavy items from the houses to the roadside. My nephew suggested we move forward and enter the town. I wasn't yet convinced it was a good idea. We stood there behind the last rubber tree before an open clearing, motionless. Watching and waiting; waiting for what, I didn't know.

With a startling roar, a camouflaged truck appeared from the east and was heading straight toward the two of us. As it rumbled closer, a soldier pushed his head out of the passenger seat window and shouted, "Soldiers on Board! "Soldiers on Board!" The truck ambled slowly along without stopping, while the soldiers with loads on their heads and shoulders came running and boarding. One soldier had so many items on his head, and with his gun dangling from one hand, he had significant trouble climbing in. His colleagues had to throw their arms around him, wrap his belongings and his large frame into one bundle, and lift him on board as the truck rolled on. We were extremely surprised; every soldier was inside that truck, none remained on the streets of Harbel. The Lord had worked a miracle with the ceasefire, just when we needed Him. Praise Him! Then, the Lord had simply removed all soldiers from our very path.

A second miracle happened the same day! Praise him! Had any soldiers remained in the area while their colleagues were stealing items from people's homes—knowing that the two of us saw the situation as we walked in—they would have killed us to maintain secrecy. Thanks to two more miracles from God, I could enter Harbel safely and search for my family without any soldiers or rebels interrogating me. At this juncture, I faced yet a new problem. I had no idea where in the town of Harbel my family was staying. My cousin, with whom my family was residing, had moved with her family to a new house when her husband was promoted in the Plantation Protection Department (PPD). I did not know their new house location.

It was time for me to strategize again. The houses in Harbel were built in rows running east and west. I decided that together we ought to search one row, walk to the end of it, and come back through the next row until we found the family or finished all the rows—whichever came first. My nephew suggested that we each take a row on our own and weave through the town separately, to save time. I objected on the grounds that we both could run off in separate directions and be lost to each other if there was a sudden shoot-out. I said we really needed to stick together to enable us also to flee together. So we carried out my plan, and within the very first row, it turned out that the last house on that street was the exact place my family had been living in! We quietly scoped the property to see if anyone was inside, until an elderly woman approached us from behind the house. She asked, "My son, who are you looking for?" "I am looking for my wife and children." "You mean the light-skinned woman with the three little children?" My heart leaped into my throat. Uncertain if I should hope nor if I should push hope down, I managed to say, "Yes. Where are they?

"Oh, young man, your children are so beautiful; I admired watching them play all the time, around here!" I couldn't think to thank her for the compliment. I couldn't afford the time.

I blurted out, "I need to know where they are!" "Can you tell me, please?"

The old woman said that the woman whom my wife and children came to live with fled Harbel on the day of the attack; of course, she was referring to my cousin with whom my wife and children lived during that time. Moreover, she said my wife had refused to join them in their flight because she didn't know where she was going. "So where did my wife go with her children, I asked the old woman quietly. I was leaning on a pole, sweat breaking out on my face. My heart was pounding. "I saw her the day she finally took her children somewhere. She was taking them to Factory C." "Where is Factory C?" Feeling sad, anxious and desperate I asked myself, "Have I taken this risk and walked here for nothing?" I became nearly full of doubt and confusion again. I had exercised so much faith to just get into Harbel, and there I was dumbly staring at this mysterious woman, feeling my faith shrink. The woman turned away from me, and I went numb.

Then, I remembered that the Lord had granted us a ceasefire when I asked him for it. I remembered the Lord moved soldiers straight off of our path. I remembered the words of the prophet Isaiah, "When you pass through the waters, I will be with you; and when you pass through the rivers, and they will not sweep over you. When you walk through the fire, you will not be burned; the flames will not set you ablaze" (Isaiah 43:2). Confidence was rekindled, God was in charge, and I was again aware that I didn't need to fear.

The old woman began walking away from us. Following wearily behind, I pressed her. "Ma'am, please— where is Factory C?"

She swung an arm carelessly off to the side and mumbled, "Factory C is that way." Her skinny fingers were pointing in the north-westerly direction.

My nephew and I started walking again, northwest toward the pile of dead, wounded bodies we had just been lying in. After a few strides I turned to look back at the woman. She had simply disappeared. We walked a few more minutes until we reached the northwest edge of town, where an automatic machine gun was resting and mounted on wheels. The gun had a cartridge almost twenty-five feet long. My nephew started walking toward the gun. I held him back by his shirt again, warning that where there is a gun, a soldier must be nearby.

"Nah. No soldiers are around here because they all went onto that truck we passed . . . remembering?"

Angry and fearful, I shouted, "Don't tell me that! Soldiers never leave a gun alone without a man to look after it!"

My nephew, a mere boy, argued, "Uncle, I swear! All the soldiers are truly gone from here!"

Without further argument, I gripped the boy's t-shirt tightly in my hot fist and guided him past the machine gun. As we walked hastily forward, a little boy jumped out of the front door of the house that stood directly beyond the gun. He was crying. The toddler only about eighteen months old, ran out and stood right next to the machine gun, continuing to sob. This little boy was my son, Papie, the childhood nickname we called him.

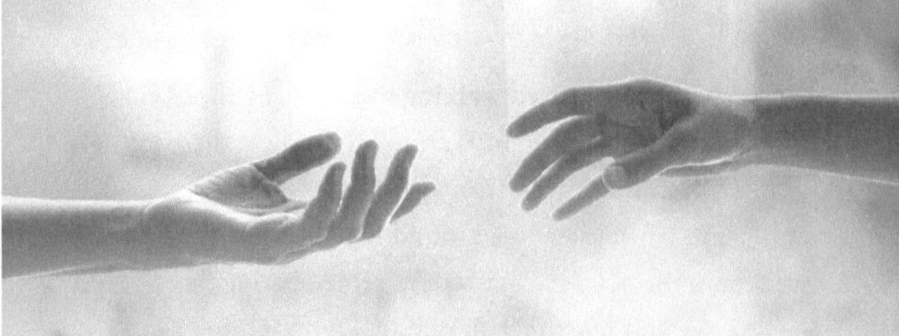

CHAPTER 5

Return Route

No longer afraid of soldiers, rebels or death, I ran to the small boy and lifted him into my arms. "Where is your mother?" I breathed into Papie's ear. He pointed to the house, where they were all apparently still hiding. I closed my eyes. My family was alive, and we were reunited.

In that moment, the two of us with Papie in my arms knelt down in the gravel before God, thanking Him for all of these miracles which brought my family back together, alive. We rose to our dusty feet again and walked into the front door. I was still carrying my son. Right inside, we found my other two sisters, Mama and Jartu, younger brother; Francis, and nieces and nephews with my wife and children.

For a silent moment, the group just stared awkwardly at me in disbelief. Then with a flurry, they all pulled themselves together and shouted in a gorgeous, chaotic chorus, "Thank you Jesus, for bringing them," "Oh, God, we thank you," "Now we know we will live," and "Thank you, God, now we know we will not die!" It was a joyous reunion.

When we entered the house, my wife ran and embraced me with such force she almost brought both of us down to the concrete floor. "How did you manage to get here?" She asked, stepping back and staring at me keenly. "I know it was God who sent you. I cannot imagine how else you could have made it here." She paused with excitement, swallowed, then her voice grew louder. "For five days we have been witnessing such terrible gun battles. We didn't know what to do or where we should go next; God must have sent you here himself!" She was rattling with both tension and relief. "Everyone left this place; some went to Buchanan, Kakata, Marshall, and other towns. I just didn't know where the kids and I were supposed to go. Praise God you came!" she nearly shouted. I reverently opened the Bible which I held in my hand all morning, gently moved the pages over, turning to Psalm 91. I read it aloud to my loved ones in the doorway, handed the Bible to my wife, and pointed to verse seven. "This was the key verse. This verse was the cornerstone of my faith, the cornerstone of my decision to take this trek to Harbel."

On the day they were leaving Monrovia, after we had prayed, I instructed my wife not to run out of Harbel when there was an attack but to find a safe place and wait for me there. I promised her that whatever happened, I would come looking for them. Narrating their circumstances, they confirmed what the mysterious old lady said to me earlier—that she had refused to follow my cousin when they left Harbel. She obeyed my instruction under those circumstances, and it worked for all of us for which I was profoundly grateful.

Mr. Cooper, a Firestone employee and the house owner had accommodated my family from the day my cousin fled. I thanked Mr. Cooper for his kindness and wished him God's blessing. My wife explained that on the day my cousin fled Harbel, she asked my wife to come along, but my wife refused her offer. My wife and I made an agreement before she left Monrovia not to run from Harbel for anything but to find a safe place to hide with the kids, and I would come looking for her no matter what happens. Mr. Cooper, who was of the Mano ethnic group, had been granted full freedom, privilege, and safety when the NPFL was in control of Harbel. But when the AFL government forces came through, his freedom was instantly gone, and he had to retreat into hiding, like the rest of my family.

So elated to finally see their dad, my immediate family wanted to open up the evening with long conversation, laughter, and telling their funny stories about the way people ran around on the first day of the attack. My children and nieces and nephews described all of the grown-ups running around as if they lost their mind, with no idea where they were going, scurrying left and right but getting nowhere. I wanted to drink in these loved ones and their every word, but I told them all that we needed to hurry. Time was a luxury we did not have that afternoon. My wife wanted to grab some toys for the children to bring on our journey. "No," I warned, "Only as much food and clothing as we can handle carrying."

"Could I follow you to at least Bahr Town village?" Mr. Cooper looked at me soberly. "And . . . do you think I will be safe along with you?"

"You are very welcome to join us, and yes, you will be safe." I lifted up the Bible again. "It is this book that brought me safely here. It is this book that will carry each of us to safety." "Onwards," I softly urged the adults, embracing my wife again quickly. "We must make haste and get out of here. We have five minutes." I started counting out loud, "One, two . . ." Then everyone from my family and Mr. Cooper began hurrying around to collect what they were able to carry on the journey. Mr. Cooper had dispatched his family away into the country long before Firestone was attacked. He was alone in his house until my family joined him.

The adults hastily discussed which roads would be best to travel on. We left the Cooper home at about three in the afternoon, Monday, June 11, 1990. Mr. Cooper along with my family walked westward on Cotton Tree road toward Division Forty-Three. All of the civilians displaced from the Roberts International Airport, Smell No Taste town, Dolos Town, Peter Town, and any surrounding villages had fled to Division Forty-Three for refuge.

We went by foot, our weathered group of old and young. The afternoon sun was brilliant, hot, and humid. The mid-dry season was just beginning at that time of year. The terrain between Harbel (Division Forty-Five) and Division Forty-Three has always been hilly, uneven, and filled with valleys and plateaus. We walked up and down, past the sprawling plantations, which sat quietly atop each plateau. Plateaus were mostly covered with the rubber trees and various landowners' plantations. The rubber trees would lose their leaves in the winter months, much like a typical winter in North America, but that day was very clear, a June day in West Africa, lush and tropical.

The two-lane asphalt pavement was extreme hot, especially as it was afternoon. My sisters had all taken off their slippers to walk barefoot, but they soon needed to put them back on. Precipitation was frequent in the plantation regions, especially during the rainy season, between April and October. But on that day, June 11, it didn't rain; the air was crisp and dry beneath a cloudless, clear sky.

Quickly I realized that my wife was not able to walk as fast as she needed to. Born and raised in Monrovia, she was a city girl, not a country girl, and she had never needed to walk more than a few hundred feet by foot. She had a load on her head that wasn't balancing well and our nine-month old daughter Linda on her back. She seemed as though she was moving one step backward for every two steps forward. I tried to plead with her gently to walk faster, or we would all be dead when a rebel force or a government force intercepted our group.

So Mr. Cooper took the load from my wife to enable us to increase speed a bit. My sister Jartu took baby Ngaynia onto her back while sister Mama carried Papie. Our oldest daughter, Jonetta, was quite heavy; even during wartime she had not lost any weight. No one wanted to carry her, so she became my responsibility. I carried her on my shoulders for the many hard miles of that journey.

We reached Division Forty-Three at around six in the evening, on the same day we had left Harbel. There we were reunited with my Cousin Sia and her husband and children. They had been living in Division Forty-Three ever since the day of Firestone's siege when they fled Harbel. We stayed together and spent the night with Sia's family, meanwhile discussing together what our departure and our trip to Bahr Town would look like. Cousin Sia and her husband agreed to leave with us at six the next morning.

Morning swiftly arrived. My cousin and her husband were not ready to go yet. We found out that they had an entirely different plan. They asked for more time, and more time still. We waited until seven and we waited more until eight. They were still not willing to leave, so we said we were heading out without them. My cousin was struggling with the thought as to whether she should follow us without her husband or not. She dreaded the thought of moving on without her husband. All of our arms were full with bundles and our own children. She wouldn't have her husband's help carrying her children, and he wasn't offering to come along—for a number of reasons. He was a city boy and a popular soccer player. There were also a lot of young women around for him to spend time with there at Division Forty-Three. He casually explained that he just didn't want to go to a small village. I tried reasoning with him, but he wouldn't listen.

I was left with no choice but to tell my cousin to just leave her husband behind, to come on this important next step with us, and I assured her we would all take turns helping with her kids and carrying one another's loads. I knew that we had the Word of God with us, the Bible; I was no longer afraid of AFL forces or NPFL forces since I had witnessed six miracles on my behalf in the past couple of days. So for the moment, I had my cousin convinced. She joined us on the road with her five kids. We had all walked about a mile together. As soon as we entered a shady grove of rubber trees she changed her mind again. "Brother, I just cannot go with you. I will wait for Frank. When he is finally ready, we'll follow along behind you." Sadly, that was the very last time I was to see my cousin. I still remember my cousin, Sia, standing on the side of the dirt road, surrounded by four kids standing and the baby tied on her back, all of them forlornly waving goodbye. We walked another forty-five minutes and reached a main highway, which would lead from Harbel to Division Sixteen and beyond. Similar to the truck we had seen passing through Harbel, this pick-up truck with two AFL soldiers in front was dropping off passengers and picking others up. They didn't ask me to show any identity paperwork, for some reason. But they did ask where our group was going. "Division Sixteen," I responded. The soldier who was seated on the passenger side in the front seat leaned out of the pick-up window and said I would owe them L$250 including loads, if we wanted their help with transportation. I paid him the exact amount, promptly, and then helped my family climb aboard. As soon as we were in, the truck took off with such a sudden and terrific speed that I thought it was going to dump my whole family right off of the back. The driver was going at least one hundred miles per hour, and the road was frightfully narrow. I was scared and asked the driver to please slow down. "I can't go any slower. It would be too dangerous as this area is so unsafe for us all, unless we speed to get through."

When we reached the Firestone Plantation Botanical Research Center at Division Sixteen, I saw one of my one of my relatives walking our way with his wife and children. They were all carrying heavy bundles on their heads. I asked the driver to stop so we could help them, too. He said this area was simply too dangerous. "We have to maintain speed to keep any of us alive,' he said. So we zipped past my relative and drove on a little farther until we reached the end of Division Sixteen and the beginning of Seventeen that would lead us to Division Twenty-One. I just couldn't wait for us to reach Division Twenty that shares a common boundary with Bahr Town.

We all helped each other and our loads off of the vehicle and thanked the soldiers. Together we walked again through Division Seventeen and on toward Division Twenty. There lay the MonroviaKanaka Highway. For anyone to reach Division Twenty-One, we all had to pass across this highway, which was literally swarming with

NPFL rebel vehicles. We stood and waited until there was a clearing in the traffic, and then we all ran across at once.

Three minutes after we crossed that highway we heard a vehicle come up behind us. They stopped at the same intersection where we were standing, perhaps a block behind us. We heard through their open window, "I think I just saw a group of people sneak across the Monrovia-Kakata highway." My family's feet all froze while each of our hearts raced in silent panic.

"You lie. No one has passed over there for a while," spoke the other man. "I'm not lying. I swear to God, I saw a group of people crossing here just now! Let's follow them and see if I am lying!" When I heard that I was terribly afraid and wished that I could slip underground. There was a profound pause for a moment; I silently glanced at my wife, my sisters and my kids. We had no hiding place. Any rubber trees and rubber bushes near the Firestone Plantation region were trimmed regularly, and cut very low and fine.

My whole being ached to simply disappear, and we almost thought we heard the sound of footsteps. Maybe they decided to come after us. Then, one of them said, "Man, don't waste our time. Let's just go!" He successfully convinced his companion and they roared off, north toward Kakata. When we finally saw their dust disappear in the distance, we all breathed a huge sigh of relief. We all knew that if they had decided to look for us, they would have found us, possibly raping some of the women and probably killing all of the men.

After another hour and a half of walking on that Tuesday afternoon, we reached our final destination, Bahr Town, my mother's birthplace, where I spent my adolescent years. This was where we planned to take refuge until March of 1991. The month of June is characterized by gradually falling daily high temperatures, with daily highs around 85F throughout the month, exceeding 89°F or dropping below 81F some of the time. Throughout June, the most common forms of precipitation are thunderstorms and moderate rain which comes in the form of flakes. Thunderstorms are the most severe precipitation in the month of June, and these occur usually at the beginning of the month. But June of 1990 was unusually dry and airy. We had seen no rain since we started our journey from Monrovia on Sunday morning, June 10. Bahr Town is situated in the beautiful Malamu and Jiplon Valley, west of the Firestone Plantation. In the south lies the Gene e Town Forest, the only tropical rainforest left in Todee District that has not been greatly affected by human activities.

My father once told me that in ancient times, the inhabitants of Gene Town were once an industrial people who had the technology to smelt iron to produce all kinds of farm tools, including machetes. They also produced gun power, he said. However, in my research in Liberian history, other sources have not produced any results to confirm or deny the existence of such an advanced society. To this day, large chunks of iron and smaller iron filings can be seen scattered under the Gene Town forest floors for miles. Also, the surrounding hills, valleys, and caves near the forest contain quite a bit.

My parents, who had been eagerly watching for us since I had paid the nervous visit to their place in Bahr Town just two days before, were so happy when we all appeared at their door. They ran to us at first sight, gripped us, and hoisted their grandchildren swiftly up into their arms. It was a moment literally spilling over with joys—a reunion of parents, grandparents, sisters, brothers, daughters-in-law, children, and grandchildren.

This was the first time that my siblings and parents and I had all been together under one roof since the day I left home for high school. The civil war had found a strange way to reunite us. The following day, my relative arrived in Bahr Town – the very relative we had seen while we sped passed him at 100 miles per hour. He told me we were extremely fortunate on the day we had passed him by; five minutes after we had cruised through, the NPFL had ambushed a vehicle just behind ours, killing all of the occupants immediately. The ambush was in Division Sixteen at the junction just before the Botanical Research Center. Apparently the ambush commander had hollered, "Many!" as our vehicle drove past. Meaning, many small children and many women were in the truck. It provided enough incentive for them to allow us to pass through.

"You were so lucky, very lucky," my other relative whom we met walking with his family and pass them had just arrived to Bahr Town. He repeated that we were lucky several times that day. "It was not luck; it was God protecting us" I gently shared my private confidence with him. We had been blessed on that journey and were continuing to experience blessings because of the protective hands of God over us. I walked quietly over to my sack and withdrew my Bible before his curious gaze. "The God of this Bible is and was our defender. God is the exact reason we did not get blown up in the ambush. It was not luck. If our pickup truck had been ambushed that day, I myself would have been the first person killed—I was seated in the front between two AFL soldiers. It's all pure miracles." I was once again amazed at God's saving grace, and I couldn't keep from sharing the stories with others.

CHAPTER 6

Memories, Clans, and Families

For the first three days, we as a family generally enjoyed resting and "being" and recovering in Bahr Town. We felt secure; it was safer there than Monrovia or Harbel. The lush rainforest surrounding the village provided ample hiding places: in caves, in clefts of rocks, in trunks of giant tropical trees. Only moments after our arrival that our children began to again show signs of carefree happiness. We were very relieved to see this. Kids often have a special way of making friends quickly wherever they go; ours were no exception. They seemed quite at home, and the fatigue, darkness, and fear of the previous few days' journeying melted away and momentarily disappeared.

I was sitting down to rest the afternoon of our arrival to Bahr Town, exhausted from the weekend's anxiety and travel. As I watched my son and daughters playing in the sand with the other kids in the village, I saw that they were entirely oblivious to any of the trouble we'd been through. Then I asked myself, what kind of world will they live in tomorrow? Will they live in peace and freedom? Then I began to reflect on memories of my childhood and of growing up in the 1960s with my paternal grandmother, who had raised me first in Careysburg; those were the times when children were children. In the Liberia of Charles Taylor, children have become grownups, committing murders and rapes.

Careysburg became the home of former slaves of prominent U.S. politicians and statesmen. General Robert Lee, leader of the Confederate Army in the American Civil War, freed most of his slaves and offered to pay the expenses for those who wanted to go to Liberia. Mr. William and his wife Rosabella Burke and their four children, former slaves of General Lee sailed from Baltimore on the Banshee with 261 immigrants in November 1953 settled in Careysburg. William Burke became a Presbyterian Minister in 1857 and helped educate his own children and members of the community. He also took several native children into his home.5

My father moved to Todee District from Careysburg when he was a young man and settled in Gene Town, a village situated one-and half miles south of Bahr Town in Todee District, Montserrado County. He met and married my mother, who was from Bahr Town. My parents lost their first set of children born in Gene Town, so Father decided after that to send my mother to live with his parents in the urban Careysburg to give birth. So I was born in Careysburg in my grandmother's home.

Careysburg was a very Americanized city, shaped by westernstyled housing and values. The inhabitants of Careysburg in those days proudly referred to themselves as "Meggin," for American. You would hear them say, "I'm a Meggin man" or "I'm a Meggin woman. They used titles such as Congress woman to address women of renown or of high accomplishment, such as women who achieved in education or in government even if they were not members of any congress. So if you heard a woman being addressed as "Con Mary or Con Jemima; for example, know that it simply means Congress Woman Mary or Congress Woman Jemima, and so on. The Americo-Liberians were proud of their American heritage, which may have been the main reason they looked down at the indigenous people so much for so long.

My paternal grandfather was a Kpelle man born and raised in *Careysburg*. He was a successful sugar cane farmer who owned and operated large sugar cane plantations on the east side of Careysburg, across the famous Kofoyah creek. Kofoyah is a creek noted for plenty of fish the locals called Kofo. . "Yah," is the Kpelle word for a body of water such as river, creek or stream. . The early settlers met at the creek, and they ate its fish and drank its water. Americo-Liberians and indigenous alike enjoyed eating kofo when cooked in pepper soup or stir fried at low heat.

My grandfather produced and traded rum, brown sugar, and syrup, and made quite a name for him. His sugar cane industry became so successful that he established distilleries in Bensonville, Todee and in the Mamba villages. Mamba Bassa people and the Kpelle people inhabited Careysburg before the American settlers arrived there. . My lineage with the Americo-Liberians came through my paternal grandmother, who was half native and half Americo-Liberian on the side of her father of Clay Ashland, Montserrado County. When my father was born, Grandma gave him her family name after the Morris' so my family carries the Morris last name. Nothing much is known of my father's maternal grandfather except that he was a successful coffee farmer and made a fortune when the Liberian coffee (coffee Liberica)6 was the leading coffee in the world market before the turn of the 19th century into the 1920s.

I was 7 years old when my grandmother brought me to live with my own parents in Gene Town. Back in the 1950s and '60s, there was a marked difference between Americo-Liberia westernized towns, such as Careysburg, and typical African villages, such as Gene Town. They were worlds apart, even if only a few miles stood between them. In any of the small Liberian villages, indigenous traditions were tightly maintained and supremely honored. I am very grateful that I was given opportunity to experience childhood in both cultures. Thanks to my exposure to both worlds, I became well-versed in both Americanized customs and traditional African values. I became fluent in the English and Kpelle languages and was pretty comfortable in the Gola language. I am deep rooted and grounded in the tradition, customs and cultures of Liberia.

Protestant Christianity was and still is the dominant religion within Careysburg and all of Liberia, for that matter. Roman Catholicism and Islam did not exist there when I was a child. They were not prohibited, but early settlers came only from Protestant Christian traditions or from various forms of secularism. During my childhood and even today, three mainstream churches existed in the town - Presbyterian, Baptist, and Methodist.

My mother hailed from the Gola people of Todee District, Montserrado County, and Bahr Town was her birthplace. She was the granddaughter of Bahr Keyan, the builder and owner of Bahr Town. Bahr Keyan's oldest son, Binda Seigh, fathered my mother with his favorite wife, Nyanie, my maternal grandmother. As a young woman, my maternal grandmother was named princess of Mombo Town, where she was born, for her striking beauty. She became renown throughout Todee District as a successful business woman and one of the first traders in Goba Town market when the market opened in the 1920s. Goba Town market was held weekly on Monday with average attendance of about three to four thousand sellers and buyers from Monrovia, Kakata, Firestone, and the surrounding towns and villages.

When I was very young, my maternal grandfather, Binda Seigh, told me the story about the origins of Bahr Town. My great-grandfather, Bahr Keyan, was an exceptional hunter, and the surrounding area and reaching as far as Divisions 10 through 43 was once his hunting ground. One day he killed such a large buffalo that all of the neighboring men brought their wives and children in for the bounty, and that hunting ground became the village named after him, Bahr Keyan Town, which now is Bahr Town for short.

In the middle of the 1960s we moved to Bahr Town, a much larger than Gene Town. Gene Town was similar to Careysburg in that my father and his half-brother, George Woodson and his wife, Aunt Matilda, had transformed Gene Town into a westernized town with the same type of housing as Careysburg except that they were smaller, flower gardens everywhere and church services were held. Bahr Town was a typical African village and life here was so radically different! There were no churches to attend on Sunday mornings, but there were other interesting activities there, which the Americo-Liberians' cities didn't offer. . I had a lot of fun living as an adolescent in that village during the late 1960s. My elementary and junior high education took place mostly at the Presbyterian Mission Boarding School nearby. I remember the Principal of the School when I enrolled there and his name was Reverend Francis R Amet. He had a wonderful family with many children two of whom were my classmates, Alex and Kofi <u>Amet,</u> from third grade to eighth grade. Rev. Amet had many daughters – Mary, the oldest; Aisha, Abram, Afi and others. He was the one of the best school administrators that the Presbyterian Church had assigned to their only co-educational boarding high school in the nation. He was a Biblical scholar and had the Old and the New Testament Bible from Genesis to Revelation at his fingertip. He was my mentor and I learned a lot from him; he and I became very close until his death. In my free time after school, I enjoyed hunting, fishing, and helping on the farm. The inhabitants of the villages were absolutely the happiest people of Liberia in those days. I honestly cannot remember seeing a person in a village that wasn't brimming with exuberance. The rainy season brought hunger every year, yet still everyone was beaming. Harvest time was especially joyful, when food was more abundant. The time of the Poro and the time of the Sande, two powerful social institutions in Liberia, were dreadful but interesting seasons for the villagers. They often involved festivities, eating, drinking, and dancing. My father loved these cultures and strongly hoped that they would continue. He and my paternal grandmother never agreed on his obsession with the Poro.

The Poro was and still is a traditional secret society which prepares tribal boys for leadership in their community and over their tribes. In the training process, boys learn to perform many rituals associated with Poro customs and traditions. Graduates are required to always respect and defend those customs and traditions, at any cost. The Country Devil is the supreme head of the Poro and his decisions for any traditional matters are final. He sets rules and enforces them. Human agents and assistants to the Country Devil, called Zoes, are believed to possess supernatural powers, and they have control over the forces of nature and the spirit world. The Zoes primarily serve to appease the spirits when they get angry, so that those spirits will in turn bring good and not harm to the community.

The Sande is the female equivalent of the Poro Society. All women in the community must be initiated, and the process begins when they reached puberty or even younger. Sande women must understand their social responsibilities as future wives and mothers. They must learn to keep secrets and be quiet, and not be given to too much talking or wine. The Zoe Gbe (Gola for "big zoe") is the "husband" to all the Sandes and is the Sande equivalent of the Country Devil. I also remembered my high-school education, which took place at Konola Academy, a Seventh-Day Adventist Co-educational boarding school, situated in Bong County, Central Liberia. After I graduated from high school, I moved to Monrovia to enroll in the University of Liberia. There I received a Bachelor's Degree in Economics.

As I reflected on the past, I drifted to sleep and knew nothing else thereafter. The next thing I heard was the voice of my mother saying to me, "How long will you sit in that chair and sleep; come in the house because it is getting late." I glanced at my wrist watch, and the hour was approaching 10:00 P.M. I had sat in that chair leaning against the wall for hours. The villagers had stopped by to greet me and left because I was in such a deep sleep that they didn't want to disturb me.

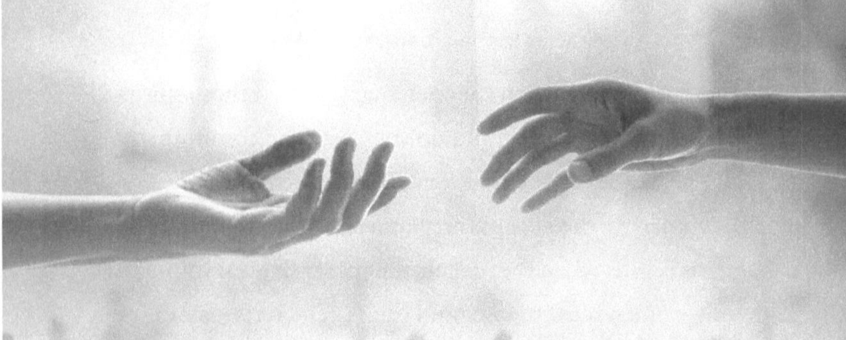

CHAPTER 7

Spiritual Warfare

The first three nights with my wife and children in Bahr Town were quiet and peaceful. We slept deeply and happily. Then, a new form of concern crept in. It was fierce and determined to replace our terror of the bullets and guns. We all had walked under a peculiar spell of nocturnal torment. When darkness fell each night, every one of us lost sleep as spiritual forces toyed with us and taunted us. It seemed clear to all of us that we were being attacked by demonic forces. Adults and children alike were woken abruptly from their sleep, crying out, scared of falling asleep again. The children became apprehensive each night when we approached their bedtime routine.

Each night, a heavy, long invisible being stood directly over my head, leaving me weak and unable to move. Other nights, it lay directly across my whole body. I would nearly suffocate, and I found it hard to breathe or move any part of my body. As this had never happened to me before, I ruled out any medical reason for the problem. I breathed freely and comfortably each night, right up until that invisible being would stand over my head or lie across my body.

Night after night I had to struggle hard to free myself from the weight, and I couldn't move any hands, limbs, or fingers. Sometimes I would just moan in a loud voice until someone heard me and ran from the other bedrooms to talk to me or even beat me in order to wake me up. The struggles continued until I started calling out the simple word, "Jesus." Or I would try to voice "The blood of Jesus!" Whenever I was able to say "Jesus" or "The blood of Jesus," I met with instant relief from the heaviness, weakness, and suffocation. The strange being moved quickly up, off, and away. Yet there were many times where I couldn't even get the words out, as the demon would be pressing on my words and repressing my ability to talk. My mouth felt sluggish and trapped. Even after I had forced my mouth wide open, it required a lot of strength and frequent attempts before I could get the whole word out, "Jesus!" Soon it became part of my night time routine to call out "Jesus" or "The blood of Jesus" whenever I had troubling thoughts before falling asleep, or when nightmares met me in my sleep. I found it necessary to keep that routine going off and on throughout the war.

Those encounters with demons have led me, later in life, to reflect quite a bit on the Apostle Paul's letter to the Romans in the tenth chapter. In Romans 10:13, it is written: "Everyone who calls on the name of the Lord will be saved." I believe this is true. Whether one is awake or asleep, this is true. Bahr Town was not a strange place to me. In fact, the very house now haunted had been built lovingly by my own father. Never was that house known to be a place where sleep was interrupted by unseen beings—until that particular week of 1990. Those demonic attacks reminded all of us that the Liberian Civil War had more than one dark side and that the war was fought on two fronts. It was fought physically with guns and spiritually with demons and voodoo. Demons were in close communication with the soldiers of that ugly war. Demons were frequently employed by the government soldiers as well as the rebels—which was why some of them displayed wicked or bizarre behaviors.

It was clear that the AFL and the NPFL signed a pact with the devil, and Satan provided their troops with bullet-proof protection through voodoo and talismans, which ritual voodoo priests crafted specifically for them to wear on their necks, legs, and thighs. As their soldiers patrolled the land, decked in talismans of all sizes, voodoo masks, or regalia, they each carried demons within and on themselves. They carried demons into every village they entered. I realized quickly that in order to survive the guns or the demons in a slaughter such as the Liberian Civil War, one must have God as his or her helper. Without faith in Jesus Christ or knowledge of His reality, one could occasionally be lucky enough to survive bullets, rockets, or grenades. But without Jesus, one could not survive the unseen forces of demons. Days and weeks passed. There, as a father in Bahr Town (no longer a junior high boy), I made a point to pray and to study the Bible daily. We instituted morning and evening family prayers—just as we had done back in Monrovia.

For some of those meetings, other members of the household or of the town would join us in our house. We'd sing hymns before going to bed; we'd sing hymns together before anyone left the house. I enjoyed sweet times of reading the Bible by myself. I came across a passage in the tenth chapter of Luke one day. Jesus was sending out seventy disciples, two by two, with power, and they were each to go on ahead of Him to the very towns He was about to enter. And when the seventy disciples returned the next day, they came with joy and said "Lord, even the demons submit to us in your name!"

According to Scripture, Jesus responded to the disciples, "I saw Satan fall like lightning from heaven" (Luke 10:18). Having read those verses, I realized that I, too, could use the name of Jesus to cast out demons. I was determined to receive and use that power during our next family devotional meeting. That evening, we gathered together the entire household—including some of the villagers—and I read the passage, giving a little talk on it. We sang the hymns and traditional gospel songs in the vernacular, and I prayed. In my prayer, I said: "I give thanks and praises to you, O Sovereign Lord; for all that you have done for my family, protecting and keeping us safe. I praise you, O God, for your power and might, your love and compassion, forgiveness, and mercy that brought us this far. I bring my complaint before you on the demons that have continued to torment us in our sleep. We are able to flee from the rebels whom we can see, but we cannot flee from the demons which we cannot see. You and only you, Sovereign Lord, can free us from both rebels and demonic forces. And Lord, please allow me to use your name and your power to cast out these forces of evil from our house so that we each can have peace. Then I said, "In the name and the blood of Jesus Christ, the Son of the Living God, I command you demons to leave this house immediately. I direct you now to go into the Pacific Ocean 50,000 miles from this village. Go into the deepest point of the Pacific Ocean and there be bound until the day when Jesus Christ will pass his final judgments over you. You will no longer come to this house to torment anybody, from this point until forever, in the name of Jesus." Then the group of friends and family there all agreed boldly and said "Amen!" in unison.

And that was it. It was finished—just as God's Word said it would be. After that evening, no one in the house ever encountered another spiritual attack or demonic visitor through the ensuing nine months we were living there. I had heard and read that when you cast demons out of a place or from a person in the name of Jesus, you must also direct them to go to a specific place. Otherwise, they would linger nearby or sneak around waiting to slip back into where they started. I was not prepared to have them around us, so I found them a new place in the Pacific Ocean and sent them into the deep. At that time when I prayed to God, it was as if I was speaking to a friend standing nearby. And it worked!

The next morning, we celebrated together and talked about the quiet and peaceful night we all had. We were sad to hear from another cousin, who came from Roberts International Airport with his family of twenty-one members including in-laws and sixteen kids. He shared that they had been experiencing attacks and sleepless night in their house ever since they moved into Bahr Town. In fact, they said, the last night was their worst night. The same thing that had been happening to me was happening to my cousin's household. I promised him we would go to their home that evening and cast out all the demons in the name of Jesus. That evening we held a prayer meeting in their house. I offered a prayer, giving the same commands I had given the evening before, in the name of Jesus. Indeed, the demons were cast out—all of them. The next day, that cousin ran over and announced to us that it was the first night they had slept well in their house since they came to town.

Our two families never experienced any more demonic visits in Bahr Town. Yes, then and now, God has given us a real power over demons and all unclean things. As it says in the gospel of Luke: "I have given you power to trample on snakes and scorpions and to overcome all the power of the enemy; nothing will harm you" (Luke 10:19).

Less than a month after our warm arrival in Bahr Town, Kakata was attacked. Kakata is Liberia's third largest city, situated about forty miles north of Monrovia. The city had changed hands many times, over the period of a few months, between several different government forces and the NPFL. The civilian death toll in Kakata was abnormally high. NPFL prevailed in the summer of 1990, took control of the city, and began a witch hunt.

When I use the phrase "witch hunt," I mean NPFL rebels would go after perceived enemies from village to village, killing men and raping the women and girls. Residents from any affected villages would run and try to hide. Hundreds of residents fled Kakata and other towns in one day, fleeing to the bushes or any surrounding villages. Mandingos, Krahns, members of the ruling National Democratic Party of Liberia (NDPL), and officials of the Doe cabinet who resided in that city had been gathered and detained or killed.

Only moments after Kakata was attacked by Taylor's freedom fighters, someone ran from our neighbor village to warn us that the residents of Goba Town (just two miles west of Bahr Town) were in flight. We knew we should flee the house in Bahr Town at that time. Together, we entered into a new life as refugees, hiding out in "the bush."

Our large group of exiled Bahr Towners rested a while in the little farm kitchen, as soon as we spotted an empty farmhouse. Then some of our friends and neighbors continued on to more remote hiding spots in the countryside. My family ran and walked, ran and walked, until we reached our own farm which was situated on the edge of a forest. We still had the family farm five miles outside of the town, where just one year earlier my father and I had entered into rice farming to grow highland rice for personal consumption and trading. A number of other

Bahr Town families chose to follow us there where we all spent a night. On the western edge of our farm was the Gene forest and Koin creek, a body of water whose source starts two miles in Division Twenty-One of the Firestone rubber plantation and runs east of Bahr Town down fifty miles to join the St Paul River to the West. For years, Koin has provided fresh water for villagers and farmers along its path.

We decided to make a large bonfire in the farmyard and camp around it. When the night grew late, people were drifting off to sleep when my father walked up to me. (He had left a little later than the rest of our group out of Bahr Town.) With serious concern on his weary face, he said "In times of war, nobody should light a large fire. In the days of old, tribal warriors followed smoke to discover hiding places of villagers. They would capture or kill them!" He took a bucket full of water and dumped it into the fire, putting it entirely out.

The women who were just about to fall asleep were startled. They stood up and asked, "What happened to the fire?" Kids and toddlers were waking up and crying right and left. I told my father that he had a valid concern and a good point, yet we couldn't just sleep in pitch darkness when we had babies and children in the group. There was a swamp very close by, which had boa constrictors and vipers. In our neighboring bushes and trees, there were many dangerous animals. Fire may be the only thing that would keep them from harming our group.

Glancing at my father's worried eyes I then gave him a steadfast look of my own. I quietly gathered some dry wood, bent down, and lit a new fire. I made it smaller than the first. In a few minutes all of the men, women, and children in the group had returned to a solid sleep, exhausted from all the running we had done that morning and afternoon except for me; I sat up the entire night keeping watch, afraid of wild beasts or snakes touching any of my loved ones. When morning came and we had assembled some breakfast for everyone, we all were able to laugh over the fire debate and over the fears we had had. And it was good.

CHAPTER 8

Humor and Fear

Friendship, nature, worship, and miracles were significant saving graces for me in 1990. But we also cannot underestimate the power of laughter. A perfect example of the healing balm of humor would be the way my relatives simply erupted with funny stories when I found them that Monday in the Cooper house. They were so quick to offer their favorite anecdotes about the grown-ups running around aimlessly when Firestone was seized.

Throughout the whole civil war, we found similar pockets of humor. There were tragic and horrid things, which took place during the war; that's without a doubt. But there was also no denying that many comical things happened. Sometimes it was just an amusing sight to watch adults run helter-skelter to find safety or shelter. The arrival of the residents from Goba Town when we were urged to leave Bahr Town is a case in point. Apparently, many families wondered why people, like my clan, fled to the forests immediately upon catching even a glimpse of someone else in flight.

It all started with a rumor that NPFL forces were approaching Goba Town one evening. When Goba Town residents heard this, they fled their town to seek refuge in Bahr Town. When Bahr Town residents heard that the Goba Town people had fled their town and were on their way to us, we fled our town and went into the forest. They slept in our town while we spent the night in the forest.

Goba Town residents asked us later, "Why did you run off so quickly?" We'd respond wryly, "Well, we saw people racing toward us; we had heard that NPFL rebels were moving this direction, and so we figured it was time for us to flee, too!" Goba Town residents would then laugh, "We came running toward you and all you could do was turn your back and run away as fast as your feet could carry you!" They laughed, we laughed, and we were all able to see some comedy in the chaos.

A similar thing occurred, a couple of weeks before, when my nephew and I were on that fateful trip to Harbel. We were outside of town and had not quite reached Harbel. When I saw a man sprinting out of Harbel with a load on his head, I asked him what was taking place there. His face brimmed with anger he shouted at me, "What? You hear sound of shooting come out of a town and you should run the other way instead, and you are moving toward it and asking me what's going on there? You stand there and ask what is going on; it is the NPFL rebels and the AFL people will tell you what is going on there. You better find your way and run."

The man was visibly angry with me for asking that question as if to say I should know better and sprinted away. That war was characterized by running. People ran and ran, not knowing where they were going; even those who never ran in their lives did. I ran, too, so many times that if the total distance I covered was to be known, it would be equivalent to several hundred miles or even a thousand marathon miles. Residents were running away from Harbel, sometimes without seeing or knowing anything that was taking place, or why. It was instinct. People would run, with adrenaline pushing them faster, at the sight of anyone else running. People would sprint, not knowing where they would end up at any sound of a gunshot. These were traumatizing times. Yet, somehow we were able to find refreshment the morning after, with a little laughter.

When we spent those few days in Bahr Town before our flight to the bush, we often heard the sounds of guns. The noise was faint and distant most of the time. Other times, though, it seemed that the gunshots were coming closer. Our level of concern would go up then, for a few hours. When things quieted down, we would return to a low-key, low-stress life again. We felt physically safe and secure in Bahr Town, overall.

When we fled Bahr Town, we stopped at a random farm kitchen to rest on our way to the forest's edge. One of our neighbors' dogs began to bark continuously. "Wow,

wow! Bow, ruff! Ruff, woof! Yap!" The slender, little dog became so incessant and noisy that we who were hiding became concerned. We asked the woman if she could please make the dog quiet, or we'd need her to stop traveling with our group. We were terrified that the barking would expose our hiding place to the rebels. The woman slapped her dog on the back as hard as she could, but still the dog went on barking. After repeated call on the woman to put her dog under control, she took off her head wrap and used it to tie the dog's mouth closed.

That was the funniest thing I had seen thus far in the war. When I saw that dog's face with the mouth tied shut and the way he was staring at me from the corner, I couldn't help but burst into laughter. My loved ones surrounding me also started to laugh. I laughed so hard that my sides hurt. Sonnie, the owner who tied the dog's mouth scowled at me and said, "You guys hush. You are complaining that this dog will expose us, but you're all being louder than the dog!" Then she turned to glance at the dog, while he sat there with his muzzle, staring at us all, and she burst into laughter like the rest of us. What a refreshing and hilarious moment that was for all of us. We needed those grace notes of hymns and humor.

Not only was there a gnawing hunger haunting me throughout the war, there was also an ongoing fear each day. Rebels were often making an intense pursuit of educated people. One day I accidentally crossed paths with a rebel commander when I was in Bahr Town. This specific commander was one I had taken great pains to avoid. We met that June when I was leaving my hiding place to enter the town, soon after the Iman had left us. "Hey, come here, come here." He gave me a stern and studying look. "You do not look like a villager. You don't belong in this town, do you?" It was a deadly accusation, one I had hoped never to hear up close.

My father happened to be standing right behind me, there on the roadside before entering Bahr Town. Fearlessly, he said in a loud voice, "This is my son! How do you expect a village person to look? Hmm? Tell me; if my own son is not from this village, where do you think this man is from? What's a member of this village 'supposed to' look like?" The rebel commander eased off pretty quickly after that. He mumbled a few things and then said confidently, "I am sorry, old man. I do see the resemblance. I will believe that you are speaking truth. But we have problems with a large number of people coming from the city of Monrovia and the Firestone Plantation headquarters, hiding in these very villages and pretending to be citizens from around here. I'm going to warn you now: if you see any of those types, bring them to me and report them to me." He turned and walked away. After that incident, I simply chose to hide myself during daylight hours while we lived on our family farm. I occasionally visited public places at night, but I spent all daylight hours in the forest, avoiding the town in the daytime as much as possible.

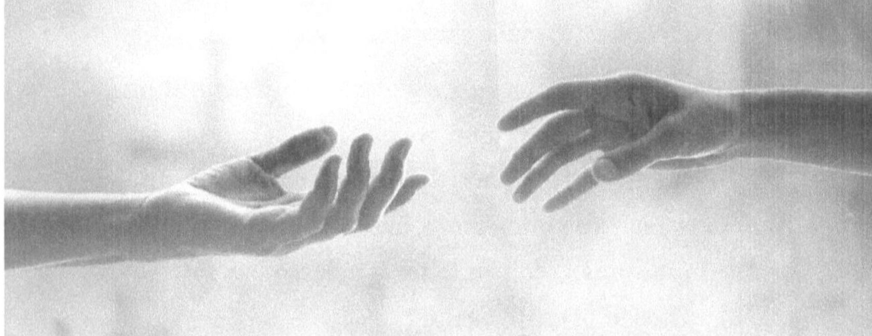

CHAPTER 9

Refuge in the Forest

Life in Bahr Town was getting normal for my little family. Everyday most people, who fled Monrovia and passed through Bahr Town, stopped with us for a couple of nights and then went on their way, seeking refuge elsewhere. Some of these people we knew and others we didn't. But we took in those who wanted to rest a while before continuing their journey. We didn't have the resources for ourselves to keep a large number of people for a longer time.

My wife and my children, parents, and siblings began to feel almost at ease in our latest home. Nestled in our town house, we were all lying in the bed one night. The children were asleep, and I was just about to drift off. At midnight, there was a knock on our front door. What came to my mind first was that the rebels were coming to get me, since they often targeted educated people. A relative of ours, Mr. Moses Washington, who was acting Minister of Information in Samuel Doe's government, had been arrested and killed by NPFL rebels while he was en route to Todee District. He had been intending to seek refuge in his mother's village. With the thought of his murder still fresh in my mind, I was terrified when I heard the strange knock on the door.

Who would knock on somebody's door at such an hour other than the NPFL rebels? I asked quietly in my mind. Rebels, by that point in history, were accustomed to hauling people straight out of their homes and murdering them just outside the front door. They would enter anybody's home anytime, day or night, and take what and who they wanted. If they wanted the wife or the daughters of that home, they got them. They were lords and law to themselves. Those were chilling and petrifying times.

We tried to respond to the knocking with a careful silence, but it became louder and more persistent. I rose to my feet and then so did everyone else in the house: men, women, and children. There were about twenty of us standing. I walked softly to the living room, reached out and held the door knob, but just before I could turn it, my father rushed to my side and held me back, electing to open the door in my place. At that time there was an unspoken rule in Liberia: one could not open the door for a stranger unless one knew their intentions and was positively certain the stranger would bring no harm. Even with that rule and guide, it was still not a guarantee that it was safe to open one's door at night. Society and people in that region had been changing for the worse in those recent months. Former friends or acquaintances were the leading cause of death in Liberia in 1990. People would often point the rebels toward where their own neighbors were hiding, causing their neighbors' demise.

My father held the doorknob and asked aloud who was knocking. Then the response came in a small, faint voice: "It is me, your friend, Molley Dukuly from Kakata." My father knew it was the voice of his long-time friend, a Mandingo and a Muslim. He was the Iman who led the weekly Friday worship service in the mosque in Kakata. We had all called him Iman Dukuly. My father quickly opened the door for his friend, hastened him inside, and offered him a seat, closing the door behind them.

Iman Dukuly has been a friend of my father for many years, dating way back to when I was a small child. He was one of his reliable and long-standing trading partners; father sold him cola nuts and he in turn sold us various household goods. Dukuly never sold tobacco products or intoxicating drinks of any kind. When he sat down with us that midnight, I examined the frail, old man with a fast glance. I had heard that it went against Islamic courtesy for one to look at a Muslim with steadfast eyes or to stare at him for long. His face and emaciated body revealed all that he had been through since the NPFL occupation of Kakata—hunger, fear, pain, anxiety, stress, and more. He was bleeding on his feet, legs, hands, and face from cuts he had sustained, apparently from racing through the bushes to get here.

However, apart from the minor cuts and bruises, he had suffered no bullet wounds. I began to ask myself, why would rebels seek to take the life of this quiet, peaceful, and innocent man? Iman Dukuly, now deceased, was unlike any other Muslim I had known. He was married to a Christian woman, Ma Fatu. As a pastor in the United Methodist Church, Ma Fatu pastored the Freeman Reserve congregation adjacent to Division Twenty-One of the Firestone Rubber plantation for many years.. Many Firestone employees living in Divisions Twenty and Twenty-one formed her weekly congregation. Iman Dukuly told my father that the people (NPFL rebels) had captured Kakata, and they were killing Mandingos. They were apparently after him also; he said to my father, "I have come to you to find a hiding place for myself, to save my life." My father patiently listened.

"All the people in Kakata are pointing out the Mandingos and giving away their hiding places. Rebels are taking homes and killing us, so there is no place left in Kakata for me to hide. Please—do this for me because we are friends!" the old man pleaded in a trembling voice. I was already deeply moved by the words of this man. My mother came out and greeted him, bowing herself a little lower before him as the Muslim women usually do. My mother was not a Muslim, but she had learned by long association that it was the appropriate way of greeting a Muslim clergy.

When the old man had finished speaking, we decided to give him a safe haven in our home. Meanwhile, the NPFL commander in Goba Town had issued a warning a few days earlier that resident found harboring Mandingo or

Krahn person would be killed with all his family members and the person they harbor because, according to them, Mandingoes and Krahn were enemies. We gave the Iman our word without a second thought, and we could not hold back on it. But by this time my faith in God was unshakable from the experience I had in Harbel.

The day my nephew and I approached Harbel, the city was in an inferno. In the chaos, God was calculating, timing, and setting into motion a series of miracles that brought in a cease fire, withdrawing the soldiers straight out of our intended path, bringing a mysterious old woman to help point the way for us, and finally leading us to the first row of houses where we stumbled upon a quiet weapon and where my son toddled straight out of the nearby door. There was also a military ambush which we passed through, unharmed, and a host of other close calls. So I had nothing to fear.

As I recalled, all of God's saving graces over those past few weeks, I certainly felt no fear about saving the life of another person in danger, if given that chance. I assured myself that the God who provided all of those miracles for me would not allow the rebels to murder us, while we were about the business of saving this kind man.

Iman Dukuly bowed his frame, his shoulders releasing a heavy weight, while his chest gave out a wheezy sigh of relief. Happiness shone from his face the moment we told him we would take him in. At that time nobody would take in a Mandingo or Krahn person even if he had been their neighbor or close friend. He murmured a few Koranic verses in Arabic and thanked us for offering him a place to live.

In order to hide his identity, my father suggested a new name for his friend. From now on he would not be called by his Mandingo name but a Kpelle name instead. My father named his friend Kollehlone, and he accepted. Kolleh is the name given to any male who is light in complexion and little in stature. Kollehlone is a light skin man. Iman Dukuly was light-skinned and small in size, so the name was a perfect match. From that day every one of us called him Kollehlone, and he answered to his new name. We constantly rehearsed the name lest we make mistake and call him by his former name. We also saw the need to keep him from public view while he did his five Muslim prayers daily.

As the days went by, the villagers were getting nervous about us. They held some suspicions and began keeping surveillance on us. They would come to our farm unannounced, pretending to be hunting. They were determined to make complaint about us for harboring a Mandingo man, but they needed proof because the NPFL Commander had also warned that if anyone said they found a Mandingo or Krahn person, they must produce the person or they would be killed.

One day I decided to confront one of those "hunters" by asking how much money he would gain if he personally reported a Mandingo person in his community. However, my father advised me to leave these "hunters" alone, to stop asking questions, so as to stay off their radar, or they would start paying more attention to me than I would like and possibly find reason to implicate me. I quickly agreed and honored that advice.

There was one evening when a Toyota bus cruised into Bahr Town. The bus driver had a girlfriend, and he came with his buddies to pay her a visit. Just a few minutes after they parked the thirty-setter bus, they had assembled a large group of villagers together and were announcing a warning. It was the same warning that an NPFL commander had sent out, earlier: "We na hear da son people here keeping Mandingo n Krahn people then! Bu way, we way con bac tomorrow when we find then, we way kay then. We way kay Dia ma, dia pa, dia wife, and dia children then all."

My father who had been present at the meeting come running back to the farmhouse, visibly scared. I had already been in bed but wasn't asleep yet. I heard my father discussed the meeting results with my mother. I stepped into the kitchen to join my parents. "Don't panic," I said. "If this warning is really true, people in the village would have already told us this. Instead, I am thinking that the visitors are making up these stories to bluff."

"No son," my father refuted. "You should not underestimate the crooks and the deception of the people in our own town." He looked exhausted and angry as he wrinkled his forehead. "Somebody must have already gone ahead and told about us—and about this man we have taken him in to provide safe haven for him. I am sorry; I can't believe what you say that everything is 'just fine!'"

With the confidence of a prophet, I looked squarely at him and said, "They will be killed on the way then. Anyone who attempts to reach here trying to kill us will themselves be killed first. That is what I believe," I said. As the bus full of rebels finally prepared to drive out of the village, they made sure to open fire before leaving. They released so many rounds of ammunition that every person in the village was petrified. Their own commander shouted to stop putting so much fear into the people, but they opted to not listen to him. The commander tried again, "Cease fire! Cease fire! Gentleman, I say cease fire!" Then they stopped.

Finally, they were quiet, the Toyota engine revved, and they were gone. Only a day later, we received news that their bus was ambushed soon after they left our village on their way to Bensonville. My father was the first person to hear about this. . When he and I had a chance to talk about it that evening, I said, "Didn't I tell you? I had declared they would die before returning to our village to murder us!" From that day on my father believed every word that came out of my mouth!

We continued daily life with Kollehlone, and developed a good routine with him on the farm. It was not a good idea for him to hang out with us in Bahr Town, so he spent his days and his nights at our farm home. Some of the villagers, especially the young men, were determined to discover the Iman's hiding place so that they could report to the NPFL and implicate us. But the area commander had warned that if any person reported that they found

Mandingo or Krahn people hiding somewhere, and if they sent their soldiers and the person could not produce the Mandingo or Krahn fugitive, they would treat him as they would treat the fugitives.

The rebels were under order to kill the person who brought in the false report if they went in and did not find the Mandingo or Krahn person. As wicked and cruel as the NPFL was, they had some strict rules that they followed. So the villagers had to make sure they saw the person physically before reporting. It was their daily routine to pass through our farm, pretending to be hunting animals, but we were intelligent to know they were searching for the Iman. Whenever we realized that they came close to his hideout, we would change his location the next hour, making it difficult for them to report anything. Our lives were in danger also because they would kill the man and members of the entire household that gave asylum to any Mandingo or Krahn.

I also learned to stay on the farm myself, and avoid the village, since an NPFL commander had once commented to me that I didn't look as though I belonged in the village. To avoid any possible chance of being "different" or suspicious, I joined the Iman, and we kept ourselves in the forest during the day. I continued hiding in the undercover of the forest alone long after the Iman had left.

The Moslem clergy was comfortable staying in the mahogany tree trunk, where he spent most of his day reading the Koran, meditating, and praying. I joined him often and spent many hours each day talking with him.

Because of the age gap between us, we had very little in common, except our spiritual journeys. I was a Christian and he a Muslim. We spent a lot of time discussing differences or similarities between traditions of the two faiths. I really learned a lot from him about Islam. In one conversation I asked the old man, "Why did you marry a Christian woman, you being a Muslim?"

"Simply because Allah is one, and humanity is one. My religion never comes between my wife and I. It is only human philosophies, which created divisions among people." He said. "We who are Muslims give our praise and worship to Allah, the Lord of all worlds, and we all give blessings and prayers of peace upon our prophet Muhammad (Sall Allahu alayhi wa sallam) as well as upon his family and friends. In fact, the definition of Islam is: 'To testify that none has the right to be worshipped but Allah and that Muhammad is His Prophet (Sall Allahu alayhi wa sallam), to establish the prayers, to give Zakah, to fast the month of Ramadan, and to make pilgrimage to Makkah, if one is able to do so.'"

As soon as we finished that conversation, he wanted to share an Islamic prayer for the both of us. We both closed the prayer together with an "Ameena!" (Amen.) He encouraged me to offer my Christian prayer, and when I was done, he joined me to say "Amen!" The Iman and I were bonded well together and became close companions in distress. He, as a Mandingo, could be an easy target for rebels and I a target for being educated. or if I am accused of being on reconnaissance. . They see me also as one who did not belong to the village no matter how I tried to behave like a villager.

Kollehlone was a gift in my life that summer, and God used that gentle man to minister to me during a trying time. Nature also ministered to me. Mother Nature had her unique way of communicating how she felt about the civil war. Nature's response to the carnage in our country was expressed in the form of dark, grey clouds covering most of the sky. Many days were cloudy and dreary —especially when there was excessive shooting or rocket launching. The birds left the trees and did not sing on those days; the creeping things went into even darker shadows. The crickets did not sound, and the wild animals that usually cried in the forest nearby at night made no sound. On those eerily quiet, cloudy days I felt especially fearful.

On the other hand, I knew it was going to be a very good and peaceful day when I heard birds singing in the cotton, oak, and mahogany trees. I knew I could stretch my knees, walk around and venture into clearings. Once the birds sang, a gentle breeze would blow, and the clouds would be softly moved aside. Whenever I heard the birds flying above, rustling in a branch, or singing in the trees, I was assured that I would live another day and not die. Nature held her own voice and her own omens. I learned a lot about the changes in the clouds and the behaviors of the animals, and reached a point where I could almost exactly predict by six or seven A.M. what kind of weather we would have that day.

As we kept the secret of the Iman to ourselves we moved him around a lot to new hideouts to keep him away from the villagers who were determined to find out our deeds, they kept increased surveillance on us. One day one of the "would be" hunters spotted the Iman in his hideout. Soon the news was circulating in Bahr Town. The town people were now getting nervous about us because they have had credible evidence to maybe indict us. Every evening, people were holding small group meetings behind houses. When they saw any family member of ours approaching their direction, the small group dispersed. I suspected that they were discussing us as to what to do in those small group meetings.

The rebels had made it clear that any citizen who brought in a report for which they could not provide evidence would receive the punishment that was intended for the fugitive. So the people in the town were in a deadlock. Who would come forward to carry the report that the Morris family in Bahr Town was aiding Mandingo person?

As tension continued to build up in the town, we got concerned but remained determined to provide the Iman a safe haven, no matter what they said or did. We had a long way to abandon this innocent man. We believed that to send him away from his safe haven meant death for him, if not from bullets, it would come from fear, hunger, or the thought of abandonment. I had no fear about what we were doing or how the town's people were thinking or planning to do. I thought about the promise Jesus made to his disciples to give them what to say when they were implicated in wrong doing by false accusers. Jesus said in Matthew 10:19 (New International Version): "But when they arrest you, do not worry about what to say or how to say it. At that time you will be given what to say." This promise was for those who are following Jesus and his will, and we were following Jesus and his will to save a life.

Meanwhile, we increased our daily prayers as tension mounted in the town, focusing on ours and the Iman's safety, asking God to provide a way out of the situation, and to ease tension in the town. We saw no need to keep the Iman in his hideout and brought him out to sit in the open with us.

Late afternoon the next day, following the evening of tension, we were all seated together in the farm kitchen, enjoying the warmth of the quiet rays of the sunlight. Then suddenly, Ma Fatu, the wife of the Iman, emerged. When we saw her approach, we stood on our feet. Ma Fatu had not been able to come to see her husband because she wanted to avoid the suspicion such a move would have resulted in the minds of rebel fighters in her vicinity. When she arrived and was seated, she said she had come to take her husband home to Kakata. The first question that I asked was "Is it safe now in Kakata?" She said the NPFL leader announced the other day that Mandingo and Krahn people should be allowed to move freely in Greater Liberia. Moreover, she said some Mandingo people had returned home since the announcement was made. We didn't hear the news because we had no radio. Any news that we heard were several days or weeks old from the day it happened. Ma Fatu explained that it was an executive proclamation from the president of Greater Liberia, his Excellency Charles Ghangay Taylor

My family received the news with gladness; it was as if a burden had been lifted. I was particularly happy that the news would ease tension in the town, which was my biggest concern. I am mindful always that whatever I do, whether good or bad, should not affect other people negatively.

Ma Fatu was a great woman of prayer, one of those we called "prayer warriors." She gave such as powerful prayer; thanking God for all that He had done for our family in preserving her husband. The face of the Iman was beaming with smiles, and he went hugging each of us, including my little children. When he got to me, both of us almost fell to the ground from the powerful hug he gave me. The Iman, who had been feeble all the time, had suddenly become energetic with such as force as to take both of us off our feet. This was a sign of the return of life in him. Praise God!

After the prayer had ended, Ma Fatu led her husband away as we followed behind and escorted them as far as Bahr Town. The couple walked fearlessly through Bahr Town before the gazing eyes of the Bahr Town people. He wanted to walk before all the neighbors' eyes, this time without fear and without hiding. It felt extremely satisfying for him to take that walk in public after all those hours of tension, fear, and torment, curled up in a cotton or mahogany tree trunk. The same evening the

Iman departed, a number of villagers stopped by to visit us in our home, something we truly were not able to allow while we had Kollehlone with us. My father, my family, and all of us agreed we would never breathe a word of what happened to anyone in the village. We would not share with our neighbors that the Iman had been hiding under our care. We felt a profound sense of release and lightness, knowing we were no longer responsible for the Kollehlone's safety or for our own difficult secret, but we did miss him terribly. He was a rare friend, and I knew he was one of the best companions God has given me for my life journey. We learned days later that it was right around that time when Taylor, head of the NPFL and the very man who triggered the first Liberian Civil War, announced that Mandingos and Krahns were granted permission to travel freely all across greater Liberia.

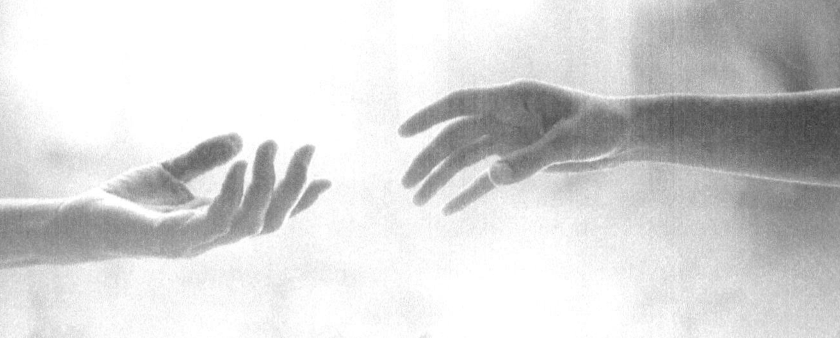

CHAPTER 10

Sustained by the Hymns, the Word of God, and Nature

In October of 1989, three months before the first civil war broke out, my father and I had agreed to begin a large rice farm operation. We were able to earmark thirty acres of high land for our family a few miles south of Bahr Town. Lowland farming was not an option for us; we lacked the expertise for that specific farming style, and we also didn't have the funds to cover the extra costs involved in laying out land for water control. I provided the sum of money for our highland operation; my father provided oversight of the manpower involved for clearing land and obtaining rice seeds.

Ultimately, we settled for only ten acres, since our region had a limited amount of seed rice available for sale that year. My father and I and the extra hands began clearing land in early December of 1989, and the project was completed by February of 1990. News of the initial rebel incursion at the north-eastern border with neighboring Ivory Coast in Nimba County did not halt the clearing and cleaning operation of our farm that summer. No one took the rebels seriously, anyway. When we arrived at Bahr Town on June 12 from Harbel, the plantings was seventy-five percent completed, and we joined in to help them plant the remaining portion.

When Kakata, Liberia's third largest city, fell to the rebels, we moved into our farm home five miles beyond the town. We still had sufficient food; including a cassava farm and gardens of eddo and sweet potato that would supply us enough food to last many months. While hiding in our forest shadows, we also had to go back and forth into the fields to carry out the planting labors. The rice planting was finished by the third week of June, 1990.

Around late June, hunger was beginning to creep in on us. Ours was a country ravaged by civil war. Every day, people from the surrounding divisions of Firestone would come by our farm, wanting to buy food from us. We sold them cassava, eddoes and sweet potatoes, yet old and new customers continued coming—and their numbers increased daily. We grimly realized that we'd have to stop selling our food as we didn't know how much longer the war would continue; we still needed enough to feed our family.

There was a morning during the very last week of June, when we woke up to find that we'd been robbed of all of our cassava, eddoes, and sweet potatoes. Hundreds of unknown people had slipped onto our land in the night, rooted each of our cassava trees, eddoes, and potatoes and carried our young harvest away. Thus began a very bleak, hungry period for our family. Within one week, we had eaten the remaining rice seed which we'd gathered during planting season. Every day in early July we had to dig through our cassava patch to find any cassavas that the thieves had overlooked. When we could not find any more leftover cassavas, eddoes, or sweet potatoes, it was still early July. We simply had nothing left to eat.

During the second week of July, my mother remembered her beans that she stored in the attic of the farm kitchen. She often planted a bit of beans among our family's rice. My mother was very industrious and was the only woman in Bahr Town who grew brown beans. She also produced tomatoes, cucumbers, okra, peppers, and bitter balls every summer. If it had been a typical summer, she would have grown, marketed, and sold those crops herself in Goba Town for a significant income. That year, though, she had kept the beans and, perhaps by divine providence in anticipation of the terrible dearth that would come upon us that year.

She had the young men climbed up and threw down one sack of the beans. Together, we cleaned the beans, removing the chaff, and they provided protein-filled meals for us for many days. Beans were usually prepared with meat and fish; luxuries we obviously did not have access to during the war. My mother had a talent, though, and could prepare the beans without meat or fish—and they still tasted fabulous. When the sack was empty, my mother called for a second sack down, and a few days later, the third sack—and that was the last. Those three sacks of beans were the only source of food for the family in July of 1990.

When we reached August, we were undergoing severe hunger, and we again had nothing left to eat. We turned to roots of all kinds from the forest. We cracked all of the palm kernels that fell from the palm trees around the farm. We ate palm cabbage yet we were never quite filled. It was not as though we had no money; we did, but it was worthless during the war. Money in Liberia had no value that year. I was often reminded during that summer of Jesus' words in Matthew:

Lay not up for yourselves treasures upon earth, where moth and rust doth corrupt, and where thieves break through and steal: But lay up for yourselves treasures in heaven, where neither moth nor rust doth corrupt, and where thieves do not break through nor steal; For where your treasure is there will your heart be also. (Matthew 6:19–21)

A person could spend their entire life accumulating wealth, but a season could come to pass when that money would only fail them, disappoint them, serve useless. That summer, adult males could not travel anywhere around Liberia, or the rebels would kill them. So, the women were the breadwinners for their families. In our family, my sisters were the income providers and shoppers during August 1990. They left each day, early in the morning, to search for food to buy. Each day they would bravely approach the rebels in Harbel or Kakata. Only the rebels and their "fiancés" had food to sell.

I would say a prayer of blessing and protection for my sisters before they left each day. I was sort-of the priest of the family. Anytime a family member was leaving the farmhouse, they would stop and ask me to pray over them. Our whole group prayed and rejoiced each evening when the women returned; we knew that many wives and sisters and daughters were not so lucky that year. Yet my sisters never came back to us actually still holding the food they had just bought; rebels along the way would surprise them, rob them, and send them on their way with little or nothing. NPFL leaders didn't provide food for their fighting men, so they stole what they could from the civilian population, taking the newly purchased clothes and food for themselves.

A strange and ironic system was that commanders of units were simply selling us the food that they stole from other neighbors along the road, and then stealing it from us again another day when we'd cross paths. With all of the injustice, still we could not dare complain. One Friday in August, I was so hungry that I almost passed out. Just at the last possible moment, my sisters returned from Firestone in the late afternoon. They immediately perceived my condition and fetched some young papaya off from the tree (the locals called them Paw Paws) and made me hot papaya soup. When I drank that hot soup, I was revived. We had not eaten the day before because we were gravely concerned for our children. Whatever purchases we had or whatever roots we found, we had tried to give primarily to our kids.

One thing that I learned could preserve me through those weeks of starvation is that I sang hymns. The hymn that ministered to me the most at this time was the hymn: "This Is My Father's World":

"This is my Father's world, and to my listening ears,

1. All nature sings, and round me rings
    The music of the spheres.
    This is my Father's world:
    I rest me in the thought
    Of rocks and trees, of skies and seas;
    His hand the wonders wrought.
    This is my Father's world. The birds their
    carols raise;

2. The morning light, the lily white,
    Declare their Makers praise.
    This is my Father's world,
    He shines in all that's fair;
    In the rustling grass, I hear him pass,
    He speaks to me everywhere.
    This is my Father's world. O let me ne'er
    forget

3. That though the wrong seems oft so strong,
    God is the ruler yet.
    This is my Father's world:
    Why should my heart be sad?
    The Lord is king; let the heavens ring!
    God reigns; let the earth be glad!"

Whenever I was painfully aware of my hunger and then sang this hymn, joy would fill my heart. I would feel as though I had eaten a balanced meal. The section of this hymn that ministered to my need most was the last stanza: "This is my Father's world, O let me ne'er forget that though the wrong seems oft so strong, God is the ruler yet. This is my Father's world: why should my heart be sad? The Lord is king; let the heavens ring! God reigns, let the earth be glad!" This great hymn carried me through the war. Each time I hear it sung, I join in praising our God—He truly did provide for my family when we had nothing on earth to sustain us.

Those long mornings and afternoons tucked within the shade and trees reminded me a lot of my friend, Kollehlone, the Iman. I missed him all the more at that point, sometimes hiding in the very same tree trunk that he had used for his secret dwelling. I struggled with some intense days of loneliness.

There was hunger, there was loneliness, and there was a gnawing terror, which was putting constant strain on my family and my personal mind and body. We faced terror multiple times each week, never knowing which horrid surprise would step around the corner the following day, never knowing who would accuse us of being AFL soldiers, and never being certain if we'd live another afternoon.

Uncertainty was eating away at us, closing in on us. Sitting under the cotton tree, sensing the unwelcome tigers of hunger and fear approaching, I would sing, "A Mighty Fortress Is Our God," Seventh Day Adventist

Hymn number 506. This was the second beloved hymn that removed my fears and emboldened me during that summer and autumn. The words were a rock and refuge:

A mighty fortress is our God, a bulwark never failing; our

1. helper he amid the flood of mortal ills prevailing. For still our ancient foe doth seek to work us woe; his craft and power are great, and armed with cruel hate, on earth is not his equal.

2. And though this world, with devils filled, should threaten to undo us, we will not fear, for God hath willed his truth to triumph through us. The Prince of Darkness grim, we tremble not for him; his rage we can endure, for lo, his doom is sure; one little word shall fell him.

3. That word above all earthly powers, no thanks to them, abideth; the Spirit and the gifts are ours, through him who with us sideth. Let goods and kindred go, this mortal life also; the body they may kill; God's truth abideth still; his kingdom is forever.

There was a line or two in all the hymns that ministered to me while I was on the run, seeking refuge. In the hymn "A Mighty Fortress is Our God," the lines, which most impacted me during my moments of fear were these: "And though this world, with devils filled, should threaten to undo us, we will not fear, for God hath willed his truth to triumph through us. The prince of darkness grim, we tremble not for him; his rage we can endure for lo, his doom is sure! One little Word shall fell him."

I chanted these words, and by the time I finished just two or three verses, I was filled with new confidence; my fears had vanished. Like all of the words of Psalm 46, Christians should have no fear "though the earth be removed, and though the mountains be carried into the midst of the sea; Though the waters thereof roar and be troubled, though the mountains shake with the swelling thereof. Selah" (Psalm 46:2–3).

By middle of September, 1990, we were beginning to see signs that the rice we had planted on our ten-acre farmland was ripening. But due to the hunger, we could not wait long enough for the rice to be fully ready for harvest. We decided on harvesting early, and the areas to start were randomly selected. We feared that if we exposed the harvest too soon, people would come under cover of darkness and harvest all the rice one night and we be left with nothing. The Firestone plantation was five miles east of our farm, and the company had stopped issuing rice to its employees, which had been done monthly since it was attacked by the NPFL on June 5, 1990. Every day, dozens of people from Firestone and the nearby villages passed through our farm, looking for a harvest to offer help and get some food.

A week later, we could not contain the crowd that came daily to our farm to offer their labor for some food. They'd seen the harvest, even though we had tried to conceal it. As we gave more food out daily, we began to pray for a miracle from God to provide food from other sources for these people. And God did just that. Few weeks into harvest, the NPFL rebels captured a ship full of rice on the Atlantic and brought the ship to the Port of Buchanan. Then they offloaded, trucked, and distributed it to the displaced and starving war victims. From the port city of Buchanan and along the highway to Cotton Tree, Harbel, Smell No Taste, Number 7, and Kakata, distribution centers were opened, serving the people in the surrounding towns and villages.

News of the rice distribution spread quickly and internally displaced citizens flocked to those distribution centers daily to get food. As that week was drawing to an end, the number of people coming to our farm to offer labor for food was greatly reduced. By the next week, we saw no one. Our farm was left to us, and the harvest was safe. The ten-acre rice farm was a source of food for many internally displaced persons from Monrovia and adjacent areas.

If God had not intervened, our rice would have been stolen, and we would have had nothing left to eat as it was with the cassava, potatoes, and eddoes a few weeks back. When the people stopped coming, we realized halfway into the harvest that the quantity of food we gave away didn't even impact the harvest at all. Even though we gave a lot of food to the visitors daily, we had more rice when the harvest was finished than we had anticipated. Praise God! He provided another source of food for the people and increased our harvest above expectation. Praise Him!

While we rejoiced that we had sufficient food to last us for many months, our happiness was short-lived. Bad news hit the family. My cousin, who had taken my wife and children in Harbel initially, had been murdered with her husband and four of their five children. Her oldest child, the boy, survived because he ran and hid himself in the elephant grass and wrapped himself with the shrubs near the spot his parents and sibling were murdered. Eye witnesses narrated the story of how they were murdered. An NPFL commander arrested my cousin's husband and began interrogating him about his tribe, where he worked, and what he was doing where he was arrested. He narrowed it down to three counts: that he was a Krahn tribesman, AFL soldier, and he had come to spy on the NPFL position to attack. So he was shot and killed for those reasons. My cousin was not supposed to weep for her husband but rather go home quietly. But she could not control he emotions and burst in weeping and wailing. So he shot her with the baby on her back and sprayed her three children that stood around her with bullets. They all perished that day.

According to the eyewitnesses, after killing my cousin and husband with the four children, the rebel was still after the little one who ran from the scene when he saw his father was shot and killed: "There was a little boy with them; where is he? I've got to get him." If anyone hides that boy from me and I find that person out, I will kay (kill) them both." Gio- and Mano-speaking residents of Division 18 came to convince the rebel commander in their language to see reason to stop hunting for the little boy since his parents and siblings were already killed. But he went on the rampage, searching for the six-year-old child everywhere. The residents tried in vain to persuade him to stop his search, saying to him, "We did not see any little boy with them." After running around the camp in a fruitless effort to find the little boy, he finally settled down. When he had left the camp and went his way, the residents went out looking for the child whom they found wrapped up in the tall elephant grass. They were trying to get hold of him, but he was afraid to come to anybody. As they moved closer to him, he ran from them. The women came out in their number to search, and he was willing to come out to them. They came, got him, and took him to the camp. A man who knew the father's relative in Harbel took the child there the next day. We didn't know anything about my cousin's murder until October 1990.

When I heard that story, I was devastated, angry, and bitter. I lamented and wept bitterly. I wanted to do something. I wanted revenge for their murder. I was planning to enlist in the NPFL myself and take up arms with the sole purpose of revenge. I wanted to avenge their murder from within the NPFL itself. Another thought was that I would return to Monrovia and enlist in the Armed Forces of Liberia (AFL) to fight against the NPFL.

That was one major reason the number of enlisted members of the NPFL was so high; people joined in to seek revenge, revenge, and revenge. If they murdered your parents, siblings, or other relatives, you joined any faction of your choice and avenged their murder. You would kill anybody who came your way. It didn't matter whether a person was innocent, or was an actual or perceived enemy.

For many months, I was angry and bitter and full of hatred. I hated everyone except my immediate family. Every day that passed, I thought of revenge and how to go about it. I didn't share my thought with my wife or my parents or my other siblings. At that time, whenever the departing words of my cousin came to memory: "Brother, you go; we will follow when Frank gets ready for us to leave this place," my anger against the rebels grew the more. At that time, I wished that I could erase the memory of their murder from my mind but that was impossible.

I could not control my emotion. I wept bitterly. I said to myself, what could I had done differently in order to persuade my cousin to get away with us. It was like the story of Lot's wife (Genesis 19:17– 26), who came halfway to escape impending doom of Sodom and Gomorrah and then returned to it. I pleaded in vain to convince my cousin to leave her husband behind and follow us to where I felt was safer. And indeed God used Bahr Town as a place of refuge for many of us who sought refuge there.

One afternoon in late October, 1990, I was contemplating on the means and method of revenge; I glanced at my children playing in the sand before me. As I sat watching them, I asked myself, what if, in the process of revenge, I get killed? What would become of these innocent little ones? And when I looked to the kitchen I saw my wife, siblings, and parents seated conversing.

Then I was grief-stricken by the thought I had and began to reconsider the idea of revenge. At that moment I repented and try to banish from my mind the thought of revenge. At that moment, also, I was reminded of the Word of God where the Lord said: "Vengeance is mine, and I will repay, says the Lord" (Romans 12:19). At that time, I recognized God, and I realized that it was not my prerogative to retaliate the evil that men do unto me or even think of retaliation. It is God's and not man's to seek revenge against another man for his evil deeds. The Bible says, "For all have sinned and come short of the glory of God" (Romans 6:35). God is the life-giver. He is also the Judge of all the earth, and he will do right (Genesis 18:25). I repented of my thought of revenge, but my anger, bitterness, and resentment still remained.

Indeed, Liberian warlords and those in government who participated in the atrocities have a lot to account for—the coldblooded murders, mayhem, rapes, and the plunder and pillage of the natural resources they squandered for their personal use and enrichment. Those who did all these evil things are getting away. So, it would seem that our siblings and other relatives were murdered in vain, and no one would come forward to say, "I'm sorry." Those who carried arms and those that gave commands to murder innocent lives have to give account of their deeds, if not before man, before God, the creator and maker of all things. If it doesn't happen on Planet Earth, one day it will happen in Heaven when the Judge of all the earth sits on his throne to judge the world (Genesis 18:25). All flesh will stand before Jehovah God, before whom they will have no executive, legislative, or judicial powers to control and contravene justice.

CHAPTER 11

Forgiveness

My entire family of five returned to Monrovia in March of 1991, at the end of the first round of fighting between government and rebel forces. A peace treaty had been signed back in August of 1990 between these forces, brokered by the leaders of the Economic Community of West African States (ECOWAS). The treaty helped to forge Liberia's interim government, which was headed by Dr. Amos Sawyer, a University of Liberia political science professor.

Upon taking office, the interim president made peace-building his priority and called on the people of Liberia to forgive and reconcile. At this time, the people were hurting as a result of the murder of their family members and the brutality they personally suffered in the hands of the government and rebel forces. Dr. Sawyer's repeated call for forgiveness and reconciliation was like falling on deaf ears. The bewildered citizens who had lost everything to the rebels wanted the AFL and rebels to renounce violence and show remorse for the harm they have done. However, that was not forthcoming as the indolent armed men and their leaders showed only pride and arrogance, having become newly rich with proceeds from the natural resources under their control which they extracted and sold cheaply. Flashy cars owned by the rebel leaders valued in thousands of dollars paraded on the Monrovia-Kakata-Gbarnga Highway daily.

At that time, the Archbishop of the Catholic Arch Diocese of Monrovia, Bishop Michael Kpakla Francis, was forceful in calling on rebel and government forces to show respect for human lives and remorse for murders and mayhem they continued to carry out all over the country. He observed that in order to receive forgiveness and be reconciled, the guilty party must be willing to admit to his guilt and ask for forgiveness. Bishop Francis was popularly known as the "Voice of Conscience" of Liberia for his stance against the brutality of the rebels and government forces. He made his called during his weekly Sunday morning mass at the Catholic church on Broad

Street, Monrovia, which was broadcast live on the local Catholic radio station and the national radio station, ELBC. On Sunday morning, hundreds of citizens attended the morning mass to hear the fearless Bishop speak against the ills in the Liberian society. And those who could not make it to the Catholic Church tuned in to the radio station to hear what the Bishop was to say on that day. His forceful and persistent message that called directly to the armed men led to threats on his own life, and he narrowly escaped death.

The Liberian Council of Churches on one hand and the Interfaith Mediation Committee, comprised of Christians and Moslems, also called for forgiveness, reconciliation, and peace among the people. My own church, the Seventh-Day Adventist Church, called on Seventh-Day Adventists and the Christian public to forgive the way Jesus did, who, when he was on Calvary's cross, asked His Father to forgive those that inflicted the pains that he suffered.

Why should I be inclined to forgive the warlords and their associates after all that they had done to my family and my nation? Not only was I waging a personal war against fear and doubt, I was also learning to fight against the demons of bitterness and resentment that were growing within my own heart. I went from loving fellow Liberians to hating them, specifically those who were NPFL loyalists, warlords, their associates, and the child soldiers. I embodied only anger and unharnessed resentment toward the rebels who had mistreated their own countrymen and hurt my family and others so deeply. I hated the AFL soldiers, especially the extremist elements in their midst, who instead of protecting the civilian population, turned against the war-wearied and defenseless citizens.

They held civilians back from leaving while attempting to flee from the city that was under attack; they shot among the crowds, killing many in their flight. Moreover, they captured hundreds of civilians and tortured, maimed, and raped women and girls. All of us were flooded with panic at the sight of a government soldier, even if that soldier was a great distance away! This type of terror, infused by the very leaders who were supposed to serve the common good, caused me to hate all the warlords, their associates, and even the child soldiers. The child soldiers were children and youth, as young as eight and nine years old, who served these militant groups and masqueraded as though they were "Robin Hood" or "Superman" and were looking out for their best interests. They were the worst of all Liberian rebels. They treated every person they encountered in cruel and in humane ways, even their own parents and siblings. It was some of those small kids who committed the worse human rights abuses the African continent had seen to date

I was an elder in my local church, and yet I was so much embroiled in anger and hate that I forgot my Christian virtues of charity, love, mercy, and forgiveness. I was supposed to reflect the love of Jesus to everyone and cater to their spiritual, physical, and emotional needs as a church elder or assistant pastor should do. Oh, no. I demonstrated nothing but hate, anger, and bitter emotions continuously, mainly because of the murder of my cousin and the personal suffering the rebels put me through. I was not in the business of going about smiling and showing kindness to people who had hurt us so much.

Sadly, I had forgotten altogether about the miracles God had wrought in Harbel to save my family. Whenever I was in the marketplace to buy groceries, I avoided sellers who appeared to be loyalists of any rebel faction. I refused to buy from them even if the goods they sold were of superior quality and relatively inexpensive. I bought from sellers who appeared neutral or who did not expressly show support for rebels even if their products were inferior in quality or expensive in price. Living in anger and hate caused me to settle for less and cheated myself of goods and services that I bought many times. I was not deterred at all in my pursuit of hate and anger toward those whom I considered to bear the greatest burden for our national woes and miseries. In 1991, the Adventist Development and Relief Agency (ADRA) International established the Liberian Country Office in Monrovia to begin humanitarian relief operations here. ADRA was among the first leading international non-profit agencies in 1990 to respond to the humanitarian crises that resulted from

Liberians fleeing from their homeland to the eastern border with Cote d'Ivoire. The Monrovia office would serve Monrovia and it's environment where over half the nation's displaced population were: Buchanan, Harbel, and Kakata in Grand Bassa, Margibi, Bomi, Cape Mount, and Lower Lofa Counties. The provisions to serve the humanitarian needs of these war victims would come from ADRA International's world headquarters based in Silver Spring, Maryland, United States and other sources.

In June 1991, I found myself working for ADRA/Liberia, having left my government post at the National Social Security and Welfare Corporation and accepted the position of associate country director of ADRA/Liberia. As a senior officer of the Adventist Development and

Relief Agency, I was faced with a dilemma. How could I bear the burden of hate and anger and at the same time provide relief to war victims, most of whom were the child soldiers and other undeserving groups whom I hated? I struggled with that for a while.

As I was struggling with my emotions, I still authorized the issuing of relief items for everyone who was in need. In my private capacity, however, and away from work, I remained steadfast in anger and hate and resentment for months. In public, I pretended to love everyone who came around me, but in private I hated some of the people.

The mass exodus of citizens from Monrovia due to the violence left few pastors to provide spiritual leadership and management of the local churches. By July 1991, some local Seventh-Day Adventist Churches in Monrovia did not have pastors; many had fled the city as either internally displaced or refugees in neighboring countries. So the Liberian Mission of the Seventh - day Adventist church then decided to look among the laymen and ordain those capable to lead their local churches. I was chosen and ordained to lead the Paynesville Seventh-Day Adventist Church in the northern suburb of Monrovia where my membership was.

At that time, the churches were flooded with new members who had received Jesus in their flight for safety. It was reasonable to estimate the growing number of new members being added to the local churches during and after the civil war by far exceeded the total membership of the Seventh-Day Adventist church of all time since 1927 when the Seventh-Day Adventist Mission was established in Liberia.

In mid-July, 1991, Pastor David Z. Whea, then Secretary of the Liberian Mission of Seventh-Day Adventists, ordained me to be the elder-in-charge of the Paynesville Seventh-Day Adventist Church. But before he laid his hands on my head to offer the prayer of ordination as they do in our church, he asked if I had anything to say. I said yes and went on to explain the emotional experience I had from the war. I let the pastor know that I was living with anger and bitterness toward those who had put us through all the pains and sufferings that we went through and still showed no remorse. I explained my struggle to show kindness, and how I hated many people.

Then Pastor Whea, an experienced church counselor, said to me, "Elder Morris, you must forgive if you would like to serve your God . . . Look at me," pointing at himself; "as old as I am; those boys tortured me at every checkpoint on the highway from Monrovia through Kakata until we reached Konola, walking on foot. I survived on thin and thread and only by the mercy of God. But I put all that behind me, and you, too, must do the same." Then he offered the prayer of ordination and the entire congregation said, "Amen!"

The moment after the pastor had finished praying and removed his hands off my head, I felt the beginning of my relief from hate, anger, and bitterness. I felt a kind of inner peace that I didn't have before, and I felt as if a heavy load on my head had been lifted. I realized that as a Christian who hate his neighbor, I was living in contradiction and hypocrisy. Having realized this, it was easy for me to repent. I did repent. Praise God, I did. It is a challenge to live among people whom you hate, and they are always there—plenty of them that you cannot avoid.

Then Pastor Itamar De Paiva and his wife, Dr. Ruth De Paiva came to Liberia to serve the Liberian Mission as president for 1991– 1992. This missionary couple and Pastor Whea were a blessing to me at that time. In a very short time, Pastor De Paiva and his wife, Dr. Ruth De Paiva had won the love and admiration of the suffering masses of the Liberian members of the Seventh-Day Adventist Church and others who were nonmembers. The De Paivas touched many lives for the better, including mine. Their workshops on peace and reconciliation and counseling helped hundreds of church members. The De Paivas now live in the United States.

Their love for the ministry and the church demonstrated an example of the love of Christ for his Church. Through the ministry of this couple, many Liberians saw the light of God's love, which led me into a deeper study of the Word of God daily in 1991 and beyond.

One day as I was reading chapter 66 of the Book of Psalms, I came across verse 18 which reads: "If I hold iniquity in my heart the LORD will not hear me" (Psalm 66:18). When I had read the text, I realized that I was holding iniquity because I was living with an unforgiving spirit, bitterness, and anger. It alarmed me, knowing that if I had continued to live this way, my prayers would have gone unanswered. The worst thing to happen to anyone is to pray, thinking that your prayers would be answered and they are not because you hold iniquity in your heart.

In the New Testament book of Matthew, the eighteenth chapter and verses 21 and 22, Peter asked Jesus, "Lord, how often should I forgive someone who sins against me, up to seven times?" Jesus said unto him, "I do not say to you, up to seven times, but up to seventy times seven (Matthew 18:21–22). Repeatedly, when I was wallowing in my anger, I had to face this tough question: how would I forgive people when they caused me so much suffering, yet they don't even think they had done something wrong? But the Lord Jesus requires me to forgive not seven times but seventy times seven, or four hundred and ninety times. He had consistently maintained that we forgive one another this number of times. You can't even exhaust 490 times forgiving any one person.

But Christ demonstrated that on the Jewish people as we read in Old Testament Book of Daniel in the ninth chapter and the twenty third and twenty-fourth verses. It reads thus:

24 Seventy weeks are determined upon thy people and upon thy holy city, to finish the transgression, and to make an end of sins, and to make reconciliation for iniquity, and to bring in everlasting righteousness, and to seal up the vision and prophecy, and to anoint the most Holy.

This is an earlier prophecy that was given to the Prophet Daniel in the Old Testament Book of Daniel chapter eight and verse fourteen which Angel Gabriel had now come to explain its meaning to the aging prophet. It reads: "Unto two thousand three hundred days, then shall the century be cleansed." According to Uriah Smith,6 the seventy weeks is a part of the 2300 days' prophecy in Daniel 8:14. This biblical scholar explains that a prophetic day is equal to a year and his stance is supported by the texts found in Ezekiel 4:6 and Numbers 14:34. So, seventy weeks of days and seventy days per week equals 490 years (70 x 7 = 490)5.

The number of times the Lord Jesus gave to Peter to forgive the one, who offends him, 490 times, correspond the number of days/years. He gave the Jewish nation 490 times to repent and fulfill the mission to the world he had chosen and ordained to execute, and they had failed.

God choose the Jewish people through whom he would accomplish his plan of redemption for the world. And he reminded them that, not because they were more in number than any other people, but they were the fewest of all people. He chose them because he loves them and for the sake of their fathers Abraham, Isaac, and Jacob to whom he had sworn, and He would keep the oath (Deuteronomy 6:7–8 KJV).

It was through the Jews that God gave the world His Word and His commandments. Isaiah declares that they were also chosen to be witnesses (Isaiah 43:10–12) through whom all nations would have relationship with God and be blessed. It was through them that He sent the Messiah, but they failed to carry out the mission for which they were chosen. Instead, they set themselves to be teachers, Pharisees, Sadducees, and scribes, and made the Word and the Commandments of God a yoke and a burden on the people. For this reason, Jesus condemned them in very strong words: "But woe unto you, scribes and Pharisees, hypocrites, for ye shut up the Kingdom of heaven against men, for ye neither go in yourselves, neither suffer ye them that to go in." (Matthew 23:13 KJV). They had a track record of failures to perform the duties they had been assigned, and yet the Lord gave those 490 years of probation to make up. Comparing this act of God allocating the Jewish people 490 years to make things right within a prophetic time period when he would accomplish his plan of redemption, and the number of times Jesus would require Peter and us to forgive one another, compels me to forgive unconditionally those who did me evil without their confessing and showing remorse. Before they asked, forgiveness is already granted. After this time, I spent the rest of my days in Liberia a free and happy man while the civil war was still raging, including "Operation Octopus" in October 1992, "Operation Grass Hopper" in March 1996, and the rest of them. Moreover, I saw and understood forgiveness on the Cross of Calvary where Jesus paid it all for me and you. In the depth of sufferings and pains, He asked His Father to forgive those that inflicted on him the sufferings and the pains that he endured. Praise God through Jesus Christ, our Lord and Savior. To Him be glory and honor and majesty and dominion forever. Amen!

CHAPTER 12

Lessons from
the Liberian Civil War

I was born and raised in the church, attended church service weekly, but I was not a devoted and praying Christian prior to the Liberian civil war. I learned to pray and became a very prayerful Christian during the civil war. The life I now live in Christ may not have been possible if this war experience hadn't happened. But thank God it did. Think about a time when you were hungry and have not eaten for many days; you have money but there was nothing to buy. You on the run and dying on your feet slowly of hunger then you gave you last prayer of hope in Jesus's name and, a moment later; the answer came when somebody unexpectedly brought in food for you as if he were sent. The Liberian civil war taught me to pray and to make my request known specifically. So throughout the war, I did not pray randomly. I prayed just for what I wanted and realized that this type of prayer is powerful; and its result is immediate.

In the gospel of Mark 10:46–52, Jesus was leaving Jericho with a large number of people following; some of them were crippled, blind, and others with various disabilities. A blind man named Bartimaeus, who was sitting by the wayside, heard that it was Jesus of Nazareth. Then blind Bartimaeus began to cry out loud and saying: "Jesus, thou son of David, have mercy on me" The people tried to stop him, but he wouldn't stop. Then Jesus ordered that they bring the blind forward to him. The people said to him, "Cheer up! Get up. He is calling you," and the blind man leaped, leaving behind what he was wearing and came to Jesus. Jesus asked him, "What wilt thou that I should do unto thee?" The blind man simply said, "Lord, that I might receive my sight." And Jesus said unto him, "Go thy way, thy faith hath made thee whole." And the scripture declares that immediately, the blind man received his sight and followed Jesus in the way. This is a typical example of specific prayer that yields immediate result. The civil war experience taught me to be specific in prayer to the things which I need. And the other piece to that is having faith in the one whom you asked. Faith was all that I had, nothing more and nothing less.

During those perilous days the prayers my family rendered to God were focused on two things: safety and food. We prayed for safety because we didn't know whether the next moment we would be dead or alive and food because we didn't know where our next meal would come from. We had money to buy anything but there was nothing to buy. Money had no value then. But

God provided our needs and to prove to me that He is El Shaddai, who abundantly blesses with all manner of blessings7 (Genesis 17:1)

I learned to ask and receive, which I dubbed "The Asking and Receiving Principle." In the Gospel of Matthew 7:7 it is written, "Ask, and it shall be given you, seek and ye shall find; knock and it shall be opened unto you." And the verses that follow, among other things, compare the giving of humans to their children with that of and God's giving to his children.

Various writers who contributed to the canon of Scripture attest to the fact that nobody on earth is innately "good" or "blameless." Yet we, who are not innately nice or good, can still give good things to our children when they ask us. How much more, then, will a righteous, kind, compassionate God give good things to His children when they ask Him? No example could support these words better than the example of the Liberian rebels themselves. Cruel and unmerciful as they were toward the general public, they were known to show extreme kindness and good will toward their immediate families and their close friends (or to anyone who had found favor or strategic advantage in their eyes). If a man capable of torturing another man can still give good gifts to his daughter or son, how much more so will our Father in heaven "give the Holy Spirit to those who ask him?" (Luke 11:13).

Better still is our asking when we do so in the name of Jesus. "And whatsoever ye shall ask in my name, that will I do, that the Father may be glorified in the Son. If ye shall ask anything in my name, I will do it" (John 14:13–14 KJV). In the gospel of John 15:16, Jesus said: "Ye have not chosen me, but I have chosen you, and ordained you, that you should go and bring forth fruit, and that your fruit should remain: that whatsoever ye shall ask of the Father in my name, he may give it you." Also, in the same of John 16: 23-24, Jesus said: "And in that day ye shall ask me nothing. Verily, verily, I say unto you, whatsoever ye shall ask the Father in my name, he will give it you. Hitherto have ye asked nothing in my name: ask, and ye shall receive, that your joy may be full."

In 1990, these Bible passages gave me the inspiration and faith to ask Jesus freely for each and every need that I faced. In the gospel of John, this principle is laid out thoroughly: The first thing Jesus wants you and me to do is to believe in him. During the civil war, I did just that—I turned to Jesus because there was no one to turn to, no one else I could fully trust. And when I turned to Him, I actually had to lean on Him for everything: for my life, safety and sustenance.

There is another aspect of asking and receiving from Jesus, which I affectionately call the "abiding principle." It is found in John 15:7 and reads "If ye abide in me, and my words abide in you, ye shall ask what ye will, and it shall be done unto you." We must be perpetually remaining in communication with Jesus, and His Word must be marinating in our thoughts and hearts before we are able to receive what we ask of Him.

According to dictionary.com, the word abide means to remain; continue; stay; to have one's abode; dwell; reside; to continue in a particular condition, attitude, relationship, etc. The part of the definition that made the most sense to me is "dwell" and "relationship". To abide in Christ means to dwell in him and to have a relationship with him. If you abide in Christ then you have taken permanent residence in Him just as an alien who is granted permanent residency in another country is allowed to live permanently in that country. He would then receive almost all the perks of true citizenship. One of those benefits when you dwell in Christ" is the liberty to "ask whatever you wish in his name, and it will be given to you. What a privilege!

The difference between those abiding in Christ and those not abiding in Him is the difference between the saved and the unsaved. When we are saved, we are described as being situated "in Christ," according to Romans 8:1 and 2 Corinthians 5:17. It is a mode of relating, in the same way that a vine relates to a branch. Without that vital union with Christ, also known as salvation, there can be no fruit borne of our daily life, no productivity. As Christ has said, without Him we can do nothing. Abiding in Christ also entails knowing him in his fullness and believing what he professes concerning himself. Jesus actually said that if we believe in him, we shall do even greater works than he himself accomplished (John 14:12)! I find that very interesting. If we can do greater works than Christ himself, that is an astounding opportunity. So then, why are we not doing these things?

Something else that Jesus really wanted to make sure we understand is that we did not choose Him; rather, He chose each of us and ordained us. Jesus said that it was significant that He chose us, rather than the other way around. "You did not choose me, but I chose you and appointed you so that you might go and bear fruit— fruit that will last—and so that whatever you ask in my name the Father will give you" (John 15:16). This shows again our innate inability to be good or do good. In our natural selves we would not choose God; it is He and only He who initiated the process of our salvation. He came looking for us to save us and give us citizenship and residency in relationship with Him.

This asking and receiving principle was what I lived by, in addition to Psalm 91, the hymns, humor, and nature during the civil war. The asking and receiving principle helped to feed my family and preserve us, and it has transformed the way I relate to God and the Bible now. My faith has increased to make me believe in Jesus and in the promises in his Word; I was able to lean on Psalm 91:7. It was that verse which gave me courage to travel across battle lines, surrounded by ruthless rebels and merciless government forces, returning safely with my whole family. I asked God in Jesus's name for a ceasefire, and he granted it. I asked Him for what I needed. He gave me all that I needed.

During those perilous days, I learned the greatest lesson of all: that there is power in the name and blood of Jesus. Make your request known to God the Father in the name of Jesus. Invoke the blood of Jesus, and the Devil will fall. He will not come after you anymore because he fears the blood of Jesus above all heavenly and earthly things. Beloved, you should be glad to know that Satan fears believers invoking the name and the blood of Jesus, and you should use that which he fears most to your advantage, and he will flee from you. It was by invoking the name of Jesus and the blood of Jesus that delivered my family. The name and the blood of Jesus were powerful even in my sleep. I a sinner used his name, Jesus, to cast out demons. What a privilege!

The next most powerful thing in my experience was the Word of God, expressed in the book of Psalms that caused the numerous miracles to take place in my war experience. God used Psalm 91:7 to show me his awesome power to deliver and to save. Psalm 91 became my Psalms of victory throughout the civil war.

The Christian hymns, songs, and the things in nature that we always take for granted have purpose in our existence. These all ministered to my family's needs. I didn't go a day without humming or singing a hymns and songs quietly, and they ministered to me greatly. There was a hymn to cast away my fears, and there was a hymn to take away my hunger. Whenever I was afraid or unsure whether I would live to see the next moment I used the hymn "A Mighty Fortress is our God" and it gave me the courage and steadfastness I needed to move on.

There were times when a small amount of food was available but not enough to go around or satisfy everyone's need; it took me only a prayer over the little quantity that I received to make me feel like I had had a full, balanced meal. The hymn, "This is My Father's World" was a "supplemental meal" whenever I was hungry and hummed it; it was like I was full. God had many ways of sustaining my family, and this was just one of them.

Up to that point, I never imagined that nature, I mean the things around us, could minister to my needs in so a profound and remarkable way. I learned to read and to decipher nature's every response to the carnage that we experienced daily and took precaution during those trying moments. Whenever the sky grew dark and fast-moving gray clouds started to form in the sky, it showed danger was imminent. During such times, the birds would hush their singing and stopped flying in the air, and the creeping things on the forest floor became silent altogether. The wind also would stop blowing so that the leaves on the trees became still. What followed those signs were sounds of heavy guns and explosions and rumors of death and destruction. When nature revealed those signs I would caution the women, who were our bread winners, not to travel outside of our home those times.

God is faithful to his Word. He says in Isaiah 43:2: "When you pass through the waters, I will be with you; and when you pass through the rivers, they will not sweep over you. When you walk through the fire, you will not be burned; the flames will not set you ablaze," God means everything he states in these verses and I am a witness.

One other lesson from the war is the blessing of promise keeping. There was a group of men who organized and called themselves Promise Keepers. These men inspired me so much and I used to admired them. I was greatly influenced by their testimonies. I no longer hear much about them. I am a promise keep myself and I have always kept my promise. I have kept the promise I made to my wife and I have never deviated. She trusted me for it and so obeyed my word when I was sending them to Harbel to live with my cousin and her family. I said to that morning of departure not to run from Harbel but to wait for me if there was an attack. I told I would come looking for her and the children. It worked fine for all of us that my wife never left Harbel until I got there and took them out. Husbands and wives should keep their vows and the promises they make to each other. God uses their faithfulness and commitment to bless them. Many marriages have failed because of broken promises which led to mistrust. You promised something and don't fulfill will lead to your next promises not to be taken seriously. It ruins families.

I was owed a friend some money and the payment due date was nearing. It was getting embarrassed that I would be unable to get the amount to pay back on the due date. I feared losing my credibility and respect and I began to worry. I said to myself, "I think I am heading for a disgrace." A few days to the payment due date, I went on my knees to pray to ask God for help. I was on my knees for a while. And after praying, I opened the

New International Version of the Holy Bible and it opened straight to Isaiah 54. As I began reading, I was startled by verse which reads: "Do not be afraid; you will not be put to shame. Do not fear disgrace; you will not be humiliated. You will forget the shame of your youth and remember no more the reproach of your widowhood." What an answer to prayer! I was afraid of losing my credibility and respect, hence, a disgrace, if I did not come up with the payment on the due date. God is assuring me that I would not be put to shame, and I should not fear disgrace. But the part that I did not understand was that of the widowhood. I said to God I am not a widower and how does this apply to me? Then I remember the story of the widow recorded in 2 Kings 4:1-7 whose deceased husband was a Priest of God and the creditors were coming to take her two sons to sell to pay the debts he owed them prior to his death. The widow went to Elisha, the Prophet of God who told her what to do. God increased the little oil the widow had in her house to fill all the vessels that she had in her house plus all the ones that she borrowed from her neighbor's until there were no more vessels to contain the surplus oil. She sold the oil, paid off the debts and she and her sons lived on the rests of the money indefinitely. I claimed the promise in Isaiah 54:4 immediately and thanked God for leading me to this passage of Scriptures.

Right away, I called my wife and explained to her my experience with the Word of God, giving this passage and the circumstance under which I came across it. All she could say was "Amen! A before the due date, I got the full amount of money I needed to pay the debt. I paid back my friend the full amount of what I owed him on the due date. Friends, God's word can be trusted. We humans are troubled about many things. We are troubled by those things that we have control over and we are troubled also by those things we do not have control over.

Jesus said in John 14:1 "Let not your heart be troubled, ye believe in God, believe also in me". If God's people would trust and believe in His Word and not doubt, they would be worry-free, and life would be a lot easier and better for all. They would be free from anxiety, stress, heart disease, mental health, insomnia, hypertension, and

free from all other psychosomatic diseases that plague the world today. The Apostle Paul reminds us: "For God hath not given us the spirit of fear, but of power, and of love, and of a sound mind." (1 Timothy1:7). If we believe in this, without any doubt, we will have peace with God, with ourselves and with our fellowmen.

I overcame my hatred and bitterness because they were robbing me of peace and happiness. I realized that I could not go on living normal life if I cannot forgive those that had wronged me. I could not go on living normal life if I cannot love those that I hated. When I finally let go of the hate and bitter emotions caused by the war, a burden was lifted, and I was set free. Praise God!

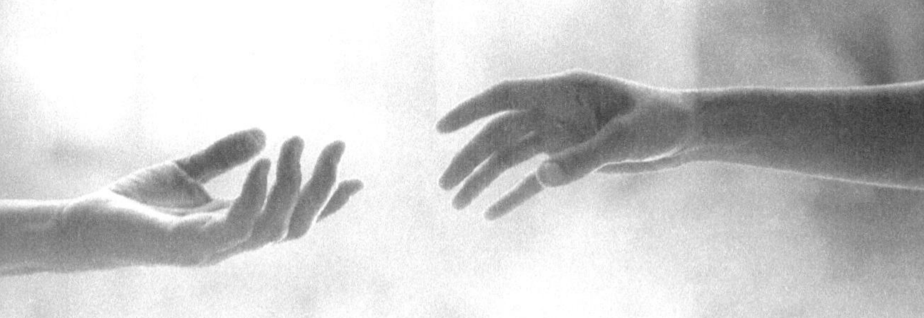

BIBLIOGRAPHY

1. Cassell, C. Abayomi. *History of the First African Republic* New York, Fountain Head, Inc. 1970

2. Ellis, Stephen. The Mark of Anarchy The Destruction of *Liberia and the Religious Dimension of an African Civil War*, 2nd Edition, New York. New York University Press 2006

3. Guanna, Joseph Saye. *Liberian History up to 1847* New York S.N Publisher 1983

4. Karnga, Abayomi. *History of Liberia* Liverpool D.H. Tyte & Co. 1926

5. Smith, Uriah. *Daniel and the Revelation* Hagerstown Review and Herald Publishing Association 2006

6. The African Repository and Colonial Journal Robert Lee's *Former Slaves Go to Liberia* Vol. 30 No. 1 1854 P.193

7. http://www.parentcompany.com/awareness_of_god/nog6.htm (2003) El Shaddai the name of God Retrieved on 05/08/2017